THE PIPER CAME TO OUR TOWN

BAGPIPE FOLKLORE LEGENDS & FAIRY TALES

EDITED BY
JOANNE ASALA

The Piper Came to Our Town: Bagpipe Folklore, Legends & Fairy Tales

ISBN 10: 1-880954-03-6
ISBN 13: 978-1-880954-03-4

Kalevala Books
An Imprint of
Compass Rose Technologies, Inc.
PO Box 409095
Chicago, IL 60640
www.CompassRose.com

Cover illustration: *The Bagpiper;* detail from an engraving by Albrecht Dürer (1471–1528). Image courtesy the United States Library of Congress Prints and Photographs Division, LC-USZ62-84266.

Back cover illustration: *An old Irish bag-pipe, once popular in the Emerald Isle, in a home in Cork, Ireland;* detail from an Underwood & Underwood stereo card, 1904. Image courtesy the United States Library of Congress Prints and Photographs Division, LC-USZ62-67034.

The poems on pages four, two hundred and forty, and the back cover are from *The Highland Bagpipe* by William Manson, 1901.

—❖—

For my father, Ronald Asala,
who read Peter Pan to me when I was a child
and opened up a world of dreams.
I miss you, Dad.

Contents

The Piper and the Pooka of November

The only tune that Rory MacCathian could play was *An Rogaire Dubh*, "The Black Rogue." He would hold himself straight and fill the elk hide bag of his pipes with air; then he would play it loud and bold or, if he was in the right mood, he could play it soft and slow like a lullaby. He played it to the best of his ability and on every occasion that presented itself—and there were many. Rory used to earn his living by playing for the lords and kings of his province. How they loved to make sport of the funny little man! But he never seemed to take mind or even notice.

That was Rory's problem. He was a half-fool and as dumb as a doorknob. He loved music (and who in Ireland didn't?) but try as he might he was unable to learn more than one tune, and that one tune was "The Black Rogue." Often he would play it at dances where the young girls would crowd 'round him, flashing their bright smiles and blinking long lashes over their eyes.

"Rory, Rory," they'd tease, "d'ya know 'The Wee Weaver'? D'ya know 'The Raggle Taggle Gypsy'?" Oh, Rory would grin and nod his head, blushing like the fool he was, and then he'd strike in his drones and play the requested tune. Only he'd have to break off after a few clumsy snatches. "I—I've forgotten it," he'd mumble and blush again. But if anyone requested 'The Black Rogue,' why! He'd get the best darn version of 'The Black Rogue' that money could buy!

Late one November night, Rory was walking home from a house where there had been a grand wake with dancing and music, and he was half drunk from *poitín*. It was a dark, wet night, and probably the worst time of the year to travel for, as any babe in the crib can tell you, November is the month when spooks and faeries and all sorts of *sheoguey* beasts walk the boglands. But poor Rory was far too drunk to let that bother him much.

Or so he told himself.

Weaving down the road, Rory was taking one step backward for every three forward, and singing himself a little tune. After an hour of steady travel, the deepening gloom and the cold were beginning to chill his bones, and when he reached the little covered bridge, he felt a wave of sadness wash over him. What he needed was some cheering up! He was still a good five miles from the warm hearth of his mother's house in the next village, so he decided to play himself a little tune. What tune? You need to ask? He placed his pipes under his arm and filled the elk skin bag with air.

From behind the piper loomed a dark shape. It folded its wings softly and on two legs crouched behind a rock. When it emerged again, it crawled belly to the ground on four legs. It grinned, and with its sharp teeth gleaming in the moonlight, pounced over Rory's head and landed on the ground before him.

"Rrrrrrooooaaaarrr!" it growled, and the very earth shook at the sound.

"Awk!" shouted the piper, tumbling on his backside; he stared with wide-open eyes at the great fanged beast before him. It looked rather like a wolf, or a bear, or a giant rat, or a...a...at any rate, it was quite furry. Its body was long and muscular like a cat's, but as tall as a Shetland pony's. Rory didn't think there were even cats that big in far off Africa! Light danced off the creature's huge paws and the piper saw that they were clawed. Or were they paws at all? He blinked. They now looked like webbed duck feet.

Rory decided he must have had more *poitín* than he thought.

The piper shook his head, rubbed his eyes, and looked again. His eyes were definitely playing tricks on him! The figure before him seemed to be melting, swelling, twisting in odd ways, and growing...*larger*?

"This'll do just fine!" The creature nodded with satisfaction. "Hop aboard!"

Rory found himself face to nose with a sleek, dark horse. A horse with goat horns, no less! "You can talk?" he asked dumbly.

"I must be able to, for sure it is that you understand me plain enough."

"Just what manner of *sheoguey* beast are you?" Rory trembled, unsure as to what the creature intended to do with him. He wondered if he looked like a tasty snack.

"Come now, Rory Padraig MacCathian! You know better than to ask me that! It's the Pooka I'm called."

"Pooka?" Rory repeated hesitantly.

"D'ja not listen to your grandfather's tales?" The Pooka shook his head in disgust. He sounded very hurt. "It's of the *Sidhe* I am."

"The Fair Folk," Rory muttered darkly. "That figures."

"So climb on my back," the Pooka invited.

"Ha! I'll be hanged if I will," Rory snapped and turned away from the confusing creature. But he let out another "awk" as he felt the goat horns jammed under his backside and himself tossed skyward.

He did a backflip through the air, a move he would have admired in someone other than himself, and he landed on the beast's broad back with a thud. "Better hold tight," the creature advised with a chuckle. "If you fall, you'll break your fool neck, not to mention your pipes. And what with you being such a *fine* piper and all, we wouldn't want that to happen!"

"Doom and gloom and destruction on you, you nasty beast! You sneakin' blackguard! And may the devil take you for his own. Such disrespect I've never seen!"

"Tch," scolded the Pooka as he started off, "mind your tongue, or I'll give you something to bawl about. I'll kick you to the end of next week, I will!"

"Mind your own tongue, you misbegotten devil's whelp!"

"Sticks and stones, Piper," laughed the Pooka.

Rory's befuddled mind sought some reason for not complying. He snapped his fingers and shouted, "Put me down at once! I need to buy some snuff for my mother with the money I've earned."

"Snuff!?" replied the creature incredulously. "Never mind your snuff! Just keep hold of my horns. Snuff?! Where would you be buying snuff at this time of the night anyway?"

Rory held on to the horns and tightly gripped the shaggy back with his knees. It was very hard to ride without a saddle!

He tried again to reason with the Pooka.

"Please, Your Honor," he begged, "let me down! It's a wee bit sick I am, having smoked too much, and eaten more than my fill. I'm not up for such a ride."

"Sick is it!? You drunken buzzard! Don't you even *think* of lying to me, Rory. I know you too well!" The Pooka reared up and tossed his head, as if doing a jig, and nearly knocked the frightened man to the ground. "Sick, you say? Your breath almost bowled me over from the next county, and you reek of a *poitín* still. Just look at your nose! It's as red as a turkey cock's!"

Rory fumed silently in his seat. He had nothing to say to the accusation, so he took the chance to study the creature instead. Now that he really had the time to consider the matter, as he wasn't soon getting away, the Pooka didn't really look like a horse after all. Not even a horse with goat horns! For one thing, it really did have clawed feet. (How did he ever *think* they were webbed?) And it was way too hairy to be a horse. Not even the shaggy island ponies had this much hair! It was almost like a combination of wool and feathers. Bad luck, too, for wool made Rory itch.

"Play up for me, Rory," the Pooka interrupted the piper's inspection. "Play 'The Belfast Maid.'"

"I don't know it," he grumbled.

"Come now, sure you do."

"I tell you I don't know it. I've never even *heard* it!" Rory shouted.

"Never mind if you *have* or you *haven't*," the beast looked 'round its shoulder, showing long, flat, horsey teeth in what the piper guessed was supposed to be a friendly smile. "You just set to playing your pipes, man, and I'll see to your knowing it." Rory was glad the beast's fangs were gone.

So the piper put air in his bag, muttering all the while, and he began to play music. Och! The beauty of it! The moon brightened and the stars twinkled more visibly in the heavens. The forest creatures and spirits came out of the woods, expecting to dance to the Faerie Queen's minstrels, and were amazed to see a mortal musician. Rory played on and on, tears of excitement streaming down his cheeks. At last he came to the end of the second repetition, and he let the rest of the air escape from the bag with a sigh. "Upon my word!" he exclaimed. "You're a fine music maker, Pooka!"

The Pooka said nothing, but continued to trot through a large grove of hazelnut trees and then found his way through the thick undergrowth alongside the path. The strange pair wound their way past the massive gnarled trunks of an ancient oak forest. Rory shivered; oak forests harbored pools of ancient faerie magic. He didn't like being there.

"Ummm, Mr. Pooka? Can you but tell me where it is you're bringing me?"

"There's a feast tonight in the house of the *bean sídhe*, the wailing women."

Mention of the banshees sent another shiver down Rory's spine, for he knew that the only time they appeared was when they wailed the doom for a mortal man. "And where is it that they be dwelling?" he asked timidly.

"Croagh Patrick. I'm bringing you there to play some music. Don't worry, you'll get a good price for your troubles."

"By my word, Croagh Patrick? You don't say! Why, you'll be saving me a journey to that holy mountain!" said the piper. "Old Father Michael put a journey to Croagh Patrick on me, just because I stole a white gander from him last Martinmas."

Now the Pooka increased the pace of his stride until they were fairly flying down the forest path. In fact, they nearly were, for a pair of brightly colored eagle's wings had sprouted from the beast's sides.

The pair ran across hills and over squishy bogland and through many a mile of rough terrain until they came to the very top of Croagh Patrick. Just as Rory thought for sure that they would continue running on to the moon, the Pooka came to an abrupt halt. He stamped the ground three times with a forefoot that was now a horse's hoof. There was a creak and a groan and the sound of stone rubbing against stone, and a door slowly began opening in the rock. A golden light shone out from the hillside and the shaggy creature passed through with the piper still astride his back. They came into a great shining hall, finer than the great hall of Tara an

Righ, where the High Kings of Ireland once lived.

Rory slid to the ground, pipes in hand. He was shaking and his knees felt like jelly from the wild ride. He looked about him with his mouth hanging open foolishly. In the center of the hall was a golden table, shining so brightly he practically had to shield his eyes from the glare.

Around the table was seated a crowd of *cailleacha*, old women. There must have been two hundred or more! All of them had stringy gray hair, sharp yellow teeth, and blazing red eyes. They dressed in tattered green cloaks and let out a howl that made the hair on Rory's neck rise. "Saints preserve us," he whispered as one of the *bean sídhe* stood and stepped forward. The poor piper was sure his end was at hand! He screwed his eyes tight shut and began saying his prayers.

"*Céad míle fáilte*, one hundred thousand welcomes to you, Pooka of November!" The voice was as brittle as dry twigs, but held a touch of amusement; Rory dared to open one of his eyes. "Who is this you've brung with you?"

"Only the best piper in the whole of Ireland," the Pooka grinned, causing Rory to give him a look of absolute terror.

The old woman raised her heavy wooden staff and the mortal yelped with fear of being struck for the Pooka's lie; but instead she banged it instead on the ground. Once, twice, three times she struck the stone floor. The sound rang through the room. At once a little door opened in the rock, and with a honk a snow-white gander flapped into the hall.

"By all the blessed saints of Eire!" Rory shouted. "I ate that very gander!" The piper stared at the bird and the bird stared at the piper. It was surely the same one he had taken from Father Michael. "My mother and I ate it for dinner one day, every last bit of him! The only other person who knew was Red Mary, the Witch. Did she somehow..."

The white gander turned his back to the blathering man, obviously losing interest. It waddled over to the golden table and began to clear away the plates and goblets. Occasionally, it would gobble down the last few crumbs of food.

The Piper Came to Our Town

The *bean sídhe* raised her staff again and brought it down with another resounding strike. "Rise up, musicians of the house!" she squawked. "Play the piper one of *our* tunes."

From the dark shadows of the hall figures suddenly rose. Rory had not noticed them before and rather wished he didn't see them now. They were dressed as Ireland's ancient Fianna, and they still carried their swords and shields in clenched fists. Although they moved with the grace of the living, the men had no heads. From a kettle across the hall, a kettle Rory had assumed was for cooking, rose the warriors' heads. There were six of them in all. Their eyes rolled madly about as they all began to sing together in a song worse than the howl of the *bean sídhe*. Ghouls and ghosts rose from the floor and floated through the walls to add their voices.

Rory sank to his knees. He wanted to cover his ears against the terrible racket, but knew it would probably be dangerous to insult them. No telling what they might be driven to do.

"Lovely, isn't it?" whispered the Pooka. Rory turned in surprise, only to catch the laughter in the beast's eyes. The Pooka opened a bird-beak and squawked. "They're only trying to see what sort of man you are! It's just a little scare. You wouldn't be the first to run screaming down the mountain; but relax, they are harmless."

When the warriors finished their singing, the piper stood glassy-eyed in fear. He watched as each of the bodies placed a head on its shoulders and sat with the *bean sídhe* at the golden table. "Well now, Piper," said the Pooka, giving Rory a kick to his backside, "quit your gawking man, and play up a tune. I think you owe these gentlemen some return entertainment." Rory glanced in the corner where the Pooka stood and nearly laughed despite his terror at the shaggy overgrown wolfhound with a lolling pink tongue.

"*Seadh go deimhin*," cried the *bean sídhe* with the staff. "Yes indeed, young piper! Play us a tune."

"*Seadh go deimhin*," shrieked the other *bean sídhe* in agreement. They wailed and sang in unison, clapping their hands and stomping their feet. Rory was trembling so badly that it was all he could do to fill the bag of his pipes with air.

It was but a moment that Rory stood alone, fearful of what the women would do when they discovered he was not the greatest piper of Ireland. Then he felt the Pooka's magic come over him. He glanced at the shaggy beast, only to find a sleek white cat nonchalantly cleaning its fur. Rory struck up "The Black Rogue."

As the piper played his tune, better than he ever had before, the old women began to dance. Their green robes swirled around them and their stringy gray hair flew about their heads. Faster and faster did they dance, and faster did Rory play. Hornpipe melted into reel, only to become a bouncing jig, and back to a reel. Just as it was with the tune "The Belfast Maid," Rory had never even heard these tunes before. He knew that it was the Pooka's magic. The piper played until one by one the ladies collapsed from exhaustion, unable to dance another step.

Then the piper played a tune he once heard from his grandfather, a slow mournful tune that was said to have been played at the funeral of Saint Patrick himself. The *bean sídhe* wailed out their sorrow, pulling on their hair and gnashing their teeth. Even the Pooka had tears in his eyes, although he hid his face behind one great wing. Rory played to the end.

"My word," said the Pooka when the tune came to a close. "Finer piping I never have heard in this world. Or," he chuckled, "in any other world, for that matter."

"If you have the magic for such music, how come you do not play yourself?" the poor man was confused.

"Easily enough answered, Rory. Of all the creatures of the world, man's form is the only one denied me. I have no fingers! Come now, ladies!" he turned to the weeping old women. "It's time to pay the piper."

One by one, each of the *bean sídhe* drew out a solid gold piece and placed it in the piper's purse, each one wiping her eyes and blowing her nose as she did so.

"By all of the blessed saints," said Rory, "I'm as rich as King Midas himself!"

"It's time to go now," said the Pooka.

"Go? Why, we've just gotten here!"

"You miserable blackguard!" he shouted, giving Rory a boot

to the rear. "*Now* you want to stay? After all the trouble of getting you here, after all of your protesting, you want to stay?"

"Well...y-yes," Rory mumbled weakly.

"Get on my back now, Rory Padraig!"

"If it's pleasing to you, Mr. Pooka, if we *must* go, I'd prefer to walk. That last ride was a wee bit much for me."

"Pick up your hat and climb up, or I'll give you a ride you'll never forget!" Rory tried to scramble up but couldn't, so the Pooka helped him up with his teeth and tossed him onto his back. Horns again sprang out of his head for Rory to hold onto. Just as they were about to leap out of the hillside, the gander flapped over to the piper and the Pooka and presented Rory with a brand new set of bagpipes.

"Och, man, I don't deserve it," tears sprang into Rory's eyes and he wiped his nose on his sleeve. "How very grand of you! It's guilty you're making me feel that I ate you for supper!" The gander merely honked and waddled away.

It was not long before the Pooka brought Rory back to the same little bridge outside of his mother's village, but not before he had run the piper over cliffs and through lakes and atop the wind. Coming to a halt, the beast tossed his head, bucked, and flipped the piper onto the ground.

"Jeez, man!" Rory bawled. "That's a fine way to treat a fellow creature."

"Go home, Rory, and quit your whining! You've come out of this thing a richer man."

"Yes," Rory considered it for a moment, "I do have a king's ransom in gold."

"Gold?!" the Pooka roared. "Is that all you can think of? You've been given two things that you did not possess before, although now I'm not so sure about the first."

"What do you mean?" the man asked suspiciously.

"You now have *ciall agus ceol*—some wits between your ears and a memory for any tune you hear."

Then the Pooka blew in his face to put Rory to sleep and disappeared with the fading stars. The last thing Rory muttered before he lost consciousness was, "Stinking rotten breath, you have...."

Rory awoke with the first pale light of dawn and stood up, shaking his head to clear his thoughts. "Crazy dream," he mumbled. He tried to walk, but his legs were light and his head was heavy, "Crazy *poitín*," he said, and collapsed back onto the ground. It was there that his eyes fell on the shiny new pipes, and the memory of the previous night came rushing back. Feeling suddenly better, he jumped up, grabbed the new pipes as well as his old, and ran the whole way to his mother's house, banging on the door as he got there.

"Mother! Mother!" he cried. "Let me in! I'm richer than Midas and the greatest piper in Eire!" When his mother did not immediately answer, he pounded again. "Mother! Mother! Come see what I have to show you!"

A face appeared in the window, an angry and sleepy face. "Go away, Rory! You're drunk!"

"I am not! I haven't had a drop to drink! At least," he amended, "at least since late last night. Now let me in!" His mother slammed the window shut.

"Hold out your apron, Ma!" Rory said when the old woman had finally dressed and opened the door. There he deposited all of the gold the *bean sídhe* had given him. There was so much gold that it overflowed her skirt and ran along the floor.

"My gosh!" she cried, her eyes opened wide in wonder. "Where in the world did you come by this wealth?"

"Not anywhere in *this* world," he laughed, helping his mother pick up the gold pieces. "Now listen here." He placed his new pipes across his shoulder. "Wait until you hear this music!" He filled the elk skin bag with air and began to play. But instead of the wonderful tunes of last night, the only sound that came from his quick fingers was a horrible howling, as if all of the screeching and squawking geese of Ireland were trapped inside his bag. The gander had had his revenge for being eaten at Martinmas!

"Stop!" his mother wailed. "Have mercy on my poor old ears!" Rory was only too happy to obey. He flung the new pipes into a corner of the room and glared at them. However, it was too late.

The Piper Came to Our Town

The awful racket had already roused everyone in the village. Some stood grumpily around his yard; others stumbled into the kitchen to have a word or two with Rory.

"I'll try my own pipes then." Rory thrust out his chin in challenge to their mocking laughter.

"What are you going to play for us then, oh Great Piper?" one of them laughed.

"'The Black Rogue'! I'll bet you anything that he'll play 'The Black Rogue'!"

"Yes, please, Rory, play 'The Black Rogue' for us!"

He turned an ear to their taunting and laughter and picked up his own pipes. Rory did not play 'The Black Rogue' as they all expected. No! He closed his eyes, took a deep breath, and clenched and unclenched his fingers. He tapped his foot in rhythm to the music of last night, humming it to himself, and then he began to play. He played every note of every tune that he played for the *bean sídhe*, and he didn't make a single mistake. Not one!

"And then there's the gold," his mother added, and showed all of the neighbors the gold she had stashed away in her apron. They would never lack for anything again!

Rory found himself seated before the fire as he told all of his excited family and friends what had happened the night before. "All while you were asleep and dreaming!" he laughed.

When she had finished feeding themselves and the neighbors, Rory's mother took another peek at the gold that was in her apron. But it was gone. Instead, she found it was full of dried and crackling leaves. "Nothing but autumn leaves," she sighed. "Nothing but a faerie trick."

Rory went to the priest of the parish, and told him everything that had happened the night before. He told him about the Pooka, Croagh Patrick, and the *bean sídhe*. But the priest would not believe one word of it. "That's a fool's tale if ever I heard one, Rory. You cockalorum! You're full of nonsense and you know it! More than likely you fell asleep under a bush and dreamed the whole episode."

"Cockalorum?" Rory cried indignantly. "Why, I'll show you!" He took out his shiny new pipes and filled the bag all of the way. The priest's study was filled with the horrible honking and screeching of geese!

"Get out of here!" the priest roared.

"Listen now to these," Rory said as soon as the awful noise died down.

"Out of here, you thief, get out now!"

Rory refused to leave and he began to play. He played all of the best known tunes of the parish and the hymns sung in church. Then he played all of the strange and fanciful tunes he had performed for the Pooka and the Weeping Women.

The magic had its effect. The priest's toes began to tap and his fingers began to snap, although he tried to hide it as he continued to look sternly at Rory. But with a happy shout Father Michael could keep it in no longer. He was up on his feet and dancing a jig on the hardwood floor. What a strange sight! Seventy-five-year-old Father Sean Micheal O'Rapherty was dancing like a young lad of one-and-twenty! When the housekeeper came into the room to see what the ruckus was about, she couldn't help but to fall a'capering, too!

Rory the Piper, as he is now known, never did get back the faerie gold the *bean sídhe* had given him, but he had an even greater treasure yet. From that day forward, there was never a piper in the whole county who could match Rory in playing. Not a one! As to the Pooka of November? The legends say that the creature only comes at one time of the year, with the passing of summer. But who can say for sure? Magic has a way of bringing about the unexpected. So if you ever find yourself walking home alone in the wee hours of the morning, be on the lookout for *sheoguey* beasts and creatures that roam the night. You just might find yourself on the back of the Pooka.

—Adapted from "The Piper and the Puca" by Alfred Perceval Graves, *The Irish Fairy Book,* 1909. Another version of the legend, translated from the original Gaelic by Douglas Hyde, can be found in *Fairy and Folk Tales of the Irish Peasantry,* selected and edited by William Butler Yeats, 1888.

Piper, Play

Now the furnaces are out,
        And the aching anvils sleep;
Down the road the grimy rout
        Tramples homeward twenty deep.
                Piper, play! Piper, play!
                        Though we be o'erlaboured men.
                Ripe for rest, pipe your best!
                        Let us foot it once again!

Bridled looms delay their din;
        All the humming wheels are spent;
Busy spindles cease to spin;
        Warp and woof must rest content.
                Piper, play! Piper, play!
                        For a little we are free!
                Foot it, girls, and shake your curls,
                        Haggard creatures though we be!

Racked and soiled the faded air
        Freshens in our holiday;
Clouds and tides our respite share;
        Breezes linger by the way.
                Piper, rest! Piper, rest!
                        Now, a carol of the moon!
                Piper, piper, play your best!
                        Melt the sun into your tune!

We are of the humblest grade;
        Yet we dare to dance our fill:
Male and female were we made—
        Fathers, mothers, lovers still!
                Piper—softly; soft and low;
                        Pipe of love in mellow notes,

Till the tears begin to flow,
　　　And our hearts are in our throats!

Nameless as the stars of night
　　　Far in galaxies unfurled,
Yet we wield unrivalled might,
　　　Joints and hinges of the world!
　　　　　Night and day! Night and day!
　　　　　　Sound the song the hours rehearse.
　　　　Work and play! Work and play!
　　　　　The order of the universe!

Now the furnaces are out,
　　　And the aching anvils sleep;
Down the road a merry rout
　　　Dances homeward, twenty deep.
　　　　Piper, play! Piper, play!
　　　　　Wearied people though we be,
　　　Ripe for rest, pipe your best!
　　　　For a little we are free.

—From *Selected Poems* by John Davidson, 1904.

— ❖ —

He bid him play a hornpipe,
that goes fine on the Bagpipe.
From the "Ballad of Arthur of Bradley"

Mannix the Coiner

Mannix the coiner[1] and Neville the piper—
    Rebels and outlaws, jolly as thrushes;
They lived in a lane where they had a great reign
    Of piping and coining, and drinking like fishes.
Neville he swore, with wild fury,
    That Mannix should share with him half the prog[2];
Then Mannix jump'd up, in a hurry,
    And sent off the wife for a gallon of grog.
"Well done!" said the piper; "Play up!" said the coiner,
    "We've gold in our pockets and grog on the brain;
The *law* and the gallows are made in the palace,
    While we, who defy them, rejoice in the lane!"

When the grog was brought in, they soon *swigg'd* it,
    And Neville then *rasp'd* up another gay tune,
And bold Mannix merrily jigg'd it,
    As brisk as a bee in the meadows of June.
"Well done!" said the piper; "Play up!" said the coiner,
    "We are the boys that can *live everywhere!*
Life, without fun, is like spring without sun—
    So we'll *flash* it away, and the devil may care!

"Those guineas—whoever may take 'em—
    Are but flying tokens to worldly fools lent,
And I am the *boy* that can make 'em,
    As bright as e'er came from the Sassenach mint!"
"Well done!" said the piper; "Play up!" said the coiner,
    "My *golden character* I'll always maintain!
And, compared with the schemers who rule and befool us,
    We're real honest men and good *boys* in the lane!"

---

1. A coiner is a maker of counterfeit coins.
2. Victuals got by begging, or vagrancy; victuals of any kind; food; supplies

Then Mannix put fire to his grisset,
    And out of his mould he shook many a *shiner*,
But ere he had time to impress it,
    In *roll'd* the peelers[3] and snaffled the coiner,
So there was an end to the piping and coining,
    And a ruction was kick'd up, but no one was slain,—
"I'm done!" said the coiner— "Cheer up," said the piper,
    "Fortune will favour the brave in the lane."

"We have you, at last!" cried the peelers,
    "Tho' many a day we have chased you in vain!"
"Then," said Mannix, "your dungeons and jailors
    May all be high hang'd—and farewell to the lane!"
Then off ran the coiner, and loud laughed the piper,
    As his friend disappear'd thro' night's darkness and rain,
Like a shaft from a quiver, he plung'd o'er the river,
    And left the bold peelers befool'd in the lane.

—by M. Hogan, from *Popular British Ballads, Ancient and Modern,*
                    chosen by Reginald Brimley Johnson, 1894.

— ❖ —

*The fyrst hed ane drone bagpipe, the next hed ane pipe made of
ane bleddir and of ane reid, the third playit on ane trump, the
feyerd on ane cornepipe, the fyfth playit on ane pipe made of ane
grait horne, the sext playit on ane recorder, the sevint plait on ane
fiddil, and the last on ane quhissel.*
**From *The Complaynt of Scotland*, 1548,
describing a company of musicians.**

---

3. A police officer.

The Piper of Weinsberg
A Ballad of the Peasants' War

The Peasants' War was a popular revolt that took place mostly in areas of what is now Germany, Switzerland, and Austria during 1524–1525. It consisted of a series of both economic and religious revolts. There were an estimated 300,000 peasant rebels and contemporary estimates put the dead at 100,000. It was Europe's largest popular uprising prior to the French Revolution of 1789.

Count Louis sat in his high-beamed hall,
Dark were the shadows that streaked the wall
And dark the thoughts that pelted down
Like stinging drops of storm-blown rain
To sere his heart with wrath and pain.

"Melchior, Melchior, play!" he cried.
The piper sprang to his master's side.
"Play me a song of laughter. Play
Till care and brooding anger fade."
And Melchior, trembling with fear, obeyed.

The notes laughed high, the notes laughed low,
But the piper's eyes grew deep with woe,
And the trembling depths of his own despair
Rushed from the pipes in a strangled wail—
And the brooding count in the dusk, grew pale.

"Hush!" and he struck the piper down.
"Go play your tune to the rabble town,
They'll add their whine as a gay refrain
To your merry melody. Now go!
Go bark with the peasant whelps below!"

Melchior crept to the great hall door,
The torch-light danced on the wide-stretched floor
And long through the quiet night, the count
Fought with the fear of a phantom sound—
A wailing of pipes that hedged him round.

Count Louis sat in his high-beamed hall,
Bright were the torches that gleamed from the wall
As a motley crowd of his merry men
Sang, while they swung and tossed their ale;
When—swift from the night shrilled the piper's wail.

Up from the valley, wild and clear,
Trembling with passionate hate and fear
It pierced like a dart. The singers hushed
Their rollicking song—they flocked to look;
And the hands that flung the casement, shook!

Their drunken eyes peered forth, "To sword!
The serfs, the serfs!"—below, the horde,
Swinging their glittering torches, wound
Like a scarlet snake up the narrow path,
Led on by the piper's song of wrath.

They tore the count from his men away,
They snatched his coat and his doublet, gay,
They stripped him clean—and Melchior bowed,
"Come, come, Sir Count! Pray dance with me,
I'll pipe for you now in a merry key!"

Two lines of spears gleamed through the night—
A glittering hell in the scarlet light—
"Dance, dance!" And the pipe's mad laugh pursued
The tortured soul of the count that fled
As the red spears tossed him overhead!

—From *Forgotten Shrines* by John Chipman Farrar, 1919.

The Piper Came to Our Town

Irish Pipers in Literature
Selections from "Irish Minstrels and Musicians"[1]

Irish-born Francis O'Neill (1848–1936) was a Chicago police officer who eventually served as chief of police for the city. He is better known, however, as a collector of Irish traditional music, stories, and histories. His works include O'Neill's Music of Ireland, The Dance Music of Ireland, Waifs and Strays of Gaelic Melodies, Irish Folk Music: A Fascinating Hobby, *and* Irish Minstrels and Muscians, *from which the following stories were selected.*

CONFLICTING INTERESTS

[There] was a County Leitrim piper, commonly known as Shaun Bacach [the Cripple] on account of his lameness. Much of his support was derived from playing the pipes at a "patron," near a prominent crossroads, every Sunday afternoon. Whether it was the charm of his music, his pleasant ingratiating manner, or the opportunity for the young people to get better acquainted, or perhaps all combined, that attracted the large attendance, rumors of Shaun's phenomenal prosperity eventually reached the ears of his reverence the pastor.

This happened of course before "patrons" and dancing fell into disfavor. Just out of curiosity, you know, the clergyman happened along one Sunday afternoon and by way of no harm stationed himself where he could keep an eye on the hole in the ground beside the piper's chair. Into this hole, in lieu of some other receptacle, the joyous swains generously pitched a coin or two after each dance.

The pastor soon was convinced that the stories of Shaun's income had not been exaggerated. To his mind, this condition of affairs could not be permitted to continue. It was positively sinful to divert to frivolity so much money needed for more serious purposes; so stepping up to the astonished piper, he told him quietly

1. O'Neill, Francis. *Irish Minstrels and Musicians*, 1913.

but firmly that he would have to leave the parish.

"Yerra, Father, what have I done out of the way at all," begged the now alarmed Shaun.

"Well, for one thing," replied his reverence, "you're taking in more money at this 'patron' than my offerings amount to, and there is not enough in the parish for both of us."

"Sure, I'm not to blame for that," protested Shaun. "'Twas your father's fault."

"My father's fault," repeated the pastor in surprise; "how could it be his fault. What had he to do with it, will you tell me?"

"He had everything to do with it, your reverence. He ought to have made a piper out of you instead of a priest!"

THADY CONNOR (AND HOW HE GOT HIS PIPES)

"Ye see, yer honors, Thady Connor (who was own brother of Maurice Connor[2] that had the wonderful tune, by the manes of which he married the grand saylady[3] of Trafraska) was the greatest piper in these parts and taught Mr. Gandsey a power of fine music; and the both of them, as well as Maurice, were stone-blind. Well, Thady's pipes were ould and cracked and had a squeak in 'em that bate the Mullinavat pig all hollow. The gentry were mighty fond of him and many a time said something about the new set they intended to get for him, but they always forgot to remember their promise, so the dickens a dacent set Thady would ever own, but for the great O'Donoghue that gave 'em to him in the ind, and the way of it was this:

"Thady, like his brother, loved a dhrop—and a big wan—and two dhrops better nor wan. And wan night he went to a wake, but went off airly, on account of a weddin' he had to be at, the morrow morning, a long way off among the Reeks.

"So to be sure, he was overtaken with a powerful wakeness and an impression about his heart. 'Arrah, what's this?' says he. 'Sure it can't be the licker, and I after drinking no more than a

---

2. See page 75.
3. Mermaid.

dozen tumblers, though I often took more.' With that he sits down by the roadside and begins to play to keep himself from sinking to sleep. All of a sudden he hears a troop of horsemen riding past him. 'A pretty set of boys ye must be,' says Thady, 'to be out this time o' night,' says he. 'Fitther for ye to be in your dacent beds than gamboling about the counthry. I'll go bail you're all dhrunk,' says he.

"Well, with that, up comes one of them and says, 'Here's a piper, let's have him with us.'

"'Couldn't ye say by yer lave?' says Thady.

"'Well then, by yer lave,' says the horseman.

"'And that you won't have, seeing I must be at Tim Mahony's wedding by daybreak,' says Thady, 'or I'll lose my good seven thirteens.'

"So without another word they claps him on a horse's back and wan of 'em lays hould of him by the scruff of his neck, and away they rode like the March winds—aye, or faster. After a while they stopped.

"'And where am I at all, at all?' inquired Thady.

"'Open your eyes and see,' says a voice, and so he did—the dark man that never saw the light till that blessed night; and meelya murther! If there wasn't troops of fine gentlemen and ladies, with swoords and feathers and spurs of goold and lashins of mate and dhrink upon tables, so broad and bright, and everything grand that the world contained since Adam was a gorsoon. 'Ye're welcome to the castle of the great O'Donoghue,' says the voice again.

"'I often heard tell of it,' says Thady, nothing daunted, 'and is the prince to the fore?'

"'I'm here,' says the prince, himself coming forrid; and a fine-portly man he was, sure enough, with a cocked hat and a coat of mail. 'And here's your health, Mr. Connor, and the health of all my descendants great and small,' says he, 'and when they're tired of the sod,' says he, 'they'll know where to get the best entertainment for man and baste, every wan, that ever owned the name,' says he.

"Well, after a while the dance began, and didn't Thady play for the dear life 'Jig Polthogue' and 'Planxty Moriarty' and all the jigs that ever were invented by man or mortal. And the gintlemen and ladies danced with their hearts in their toes.

"'Twas all very well till the ould ancient harper of the O'Donoghues asked for a trial aginst Thady, to see if he wouldn't get louder music out of a handful of cats-guts; and Thady bate him to smithereens. When the consated harper found he was bate, he comes behind Thady, and with an ould knife or skian, rips open the bag, and lets out the wind that makes the music.

"'I'm done for now,' says Thady, as he aims a wallop at the harper's head that sent him reeling along the flure. Then all the company sets up a loud *ullagoane*—the dance was over—and tells Thady he might as well go home. 'And who'll pay me for my pipes?' says Thady, who was a cunning boy after all. 'They were as good as new,' says he, 'and they aren't worth minding now.'

"'Fair exchange is no robbery,' says the prince, 'and here's a set that will make your fortune, so be on as fast as you can, for the harper is bringing up his faction, and he'll sarve you as he did your pipes.' Well, Thady made a spring to get out of harm's way, and landed in a pool of water which tilled his eyes and ears, and he heard a voice after him that he thought was the harper's, only it wasn't, but it was his wife Biddy that was waking him, as she found him asleep under the very hedge where the O'Donoghue horsemen found him earlier in the night.

"And now, plase your honor, nobody misbelieved the story he told the neighbors, because ye see the bran new pipes were to the fore; for there he had 'em under his arm, and sure how would he get 'em if 'twasn't from the great O'Donoghue himself."

DANIEL O'LEARY, THE DUHALLOW PIPER

In the early years of the nineteenth century, when the world-renowned harpers had vanished like snow in spring from the land which their art had glorified, great performers on the melodious Union pipes nourished in goodly numbers. Like the harpers, not a few of them were attached to families of wealth and distinction, regardless of racial origin, while yet others—true minstrels—led a wandering life. They were in fact so much a part of the ordinary institutions of the country that but casual and meagre references, out of all proportion to their numbers, is to be found in Irish literature concerning them, from the early centuries to the present time; and that little which has been preserved to us in print we owe, in a great measure, to travelers and writers in whose veins flow the blood of the invader.

In those days, a traveler rambling through certain wild districts in the north-western part of the County of Cork, by a curious circumstance, had the pleasure of hearing some of the best Irish airs played on the best set of "organ" pipes, by the best piper in Munster—a rare treat, as he says in a communication to the editor of the *Dublin Penny Journal*, in October, 1834.

Seated on the rampart of a rath or fort, he fell to moralizing on the past, and the people who lived and loved and died and left not a trace behind of their identity in the glorious scene before him, where the light and shade of hill and vale were beautifully linked with the evening mist that curled along the banks of the winding Araglin. When he awoke from his reverie, it was too late to reach his destination before dark, so he gladly accepted the invitation of an intelligent herdsman to partake of his hospitality for the night. As a special inducement, he was promised a rare treat of national Irish music, from the chanter of Daniel O'Leary, the first piper of Munster, who luckily had paid them a visit.

When the traveler and his host entered the cozy cabin, right beside the cheerful fire sat the piper, a diminutive man, deformed in person, like Willie Wattle's wife, who—

"Had a hump upon her breast
The twin of that upon her shoulder."

He had a knowing cast of countenance and a keen, observant eye. After the customary *"Cead mile failthe"* and the ordinary exchange of compliments, O'Leary yoked on his pipes to do the stranger courtesy, and played "Eileen a Roon" and "O'Carolan's

Farewell to Music," with exquisite taste and feeling. "I have listened to much music," to quote the traveler's words, "but Jack Pigott's 'Cois na Breedha' and O'Leary's 'Humors of Glin' are in my estimation the *ne plus ultra* of bagpipe melody."

In the course of the night the hospitable herdsman, seeing how much pleased his guest was with O'Leary's splendid performance, requested the piper to favor him with an account of his adventures with the "good people" at the fort of Doon.

"Ah!" said the piper, "this gentleman has read too much to credit such stories, though in the ancient times people saw strange sights, and seeing was believing." As the traveler loved legendary lore nearly as well as music, he requested the piper to relate his story, which was to the following effect:

One November afternoon, Daniel O'Leary was routed from his bed at his sister's house in the town of Millstreet. He had retired to take a nap, for he had been engaged during the preceding night at the Wallis Arms playing for a party of gentlemen that dined there, and had scarcely fetched half a dozen snores when his repose was interrupted. It was a message from the squire of Kilmeen, commanding his attendance at the Castle. He had a grand party, and though a fiddler or two were in requisition, Miss Julia Twomey, one of the young ladies invited, could abide no other music than O'Leary's. In fact, the estimation in which a "dinner" or wedding was held in Duhallow was regulated by the circumstances of that piper's absence or attendance there. Though our friend Daniel had no relish for the interruption of his much needed rest, he had too much respect for the squire to disregard his wishes.

After treating the messenger, he was about to mount the fine horse which the squire had sent for him, when a blue-eyed thuckeen from Knocknagrue, "an ould acquaintance" of O'Leary's, passed by, and he directed the squire's man to walk the horse slowly on before them, while he whispered a word or two to Nancy Walsh.

They entered the public house at the crossroad, and were so agreeably entertained with each other's company, over a glass of punch, that it was dark night before they parted. At length, after

The Piper Came to Our Town

taking a parting kiss, the piper pursued his way, in the hope of soon overtaking the man with the horse; but when he reached Finown, no servant lingered for him on the bank of the rapid water. Having made his way, with some difficulty, over the high stepping stones, he set forward with accelerated speed, in the hope of overtaking him before he reached Blackwater Bridge, for where the broad river rushes through the glen and sweeps the tall rock at Justice's Castle, the scene is wild and lonely, and the neighborhood of that ancient building had, time out of mind, been deemed a favorite haunt of the "good people."

As he approached the bridge, the moon was rising, and our friend O'Leary halted to hear if possible the friendly tramp of the horse's hoofs. 'Twas all in vain. He heard no sound, save the distant voice of the watchdog, and no object met his eyes by the ivied towers of the castle, surmounting the fir trees that crowned the rock, and flung their giant shadows athwart the stream beneath the pale moonbeams, that danced like things of life upon the water.

Though the Duhallow piper was "purty well, I thank ye," yet the punch he quaffed in Nancy Walsh's company could not make him scorn the dangers that superstition taught him to expect in this fairy haunt. Knowing the power of music on those occasions, he yoked on his pipes, intending to raise a sacred melody as a guard against the influence of any evil thing that might hover round his path; but owing to some unaccountable irregularity of idea, after many vain attempts, he could bring no other tune out of the chanter than O'Carolan's "Receipt for Drinking Whiskey."

This beautiful air rose sweetly on the night wind, as he journeyed along, and when the tune was nearly concluded, he thought he could distinguish the tramp of horses. He ceased his strain, thinking it was the servant that came trotting in the distance behind, but soon perceived the sound was multiplied by a hundred hoofs along the road. He could now descry the dim figures of horsemen as they approached nearer and, supposing that he had fallen in with a party of *Rockites*, he withdrew a short distance from the road to the shelter of a furze bush. As the long procession moved onward, he thought he could distinguish among the horsemen the shape of persons whom he had known to be long dead, and who, he thought, were resting in their quiet graves. But his surprise was considerably increased to behold his friend Tom Tierney, who conversed with him, alive and well, that very evening in Millstreet, in the last rank that ended the cavalcade, and to complete his astonishment, the horse on which Tom rode was drowned in a bog hole, to O'Leary's certain knowledge, about a fortnight before.

From these circumstances, the piper was now convinced that these horsemen were the *slua shee* or fairy host. Tom wore his usual broad-brimmed beaver, that saved his complexion from the summer's sun, for he always shone as a rustic dandy of the first water. The moon which emerged that moment from behind a cloud gleamed on the large gold ring that circled his forefinger, and which Tom on all occasions took no small pains to display, for it descended to him through a long line of ancestry from the sister of Dhonal Caum, whose descendent he was.

"A virrah dheelish! Is it dhramin' I am, or are my eyes desaving me all out?" says the astonished piper.

"Tom Tierney, if it's yourself that's there, wouldn't you spake to the son of your own blood relation and not lave him to die with the cowld without the benefit of the clargy by the roadside?"

"Ayeh! it's a bad day I wouldn't do more nor that," says Tom, spurring his horse into the ditch to enable the piper to mount behind him with facility, and at that moment a peal of laughter ran through the whole troop. Had the explorer of an ancient catacomb heard the dead of a thousand years bid him welcome to their silent mansions, he could not have experienced greater fear than did O'Leary, when this wild burst of unnatural mirth rose from the ranks of the strange cavalcade upon his mortal ear.

After mounting, his fear was further increased to find that neither the horse nor the rider had the solidity of frame common to mere matter; in short, they seemed to form an indefinable something between the shadow and substance of bodies.

When they came to the crossroad that led to the squire's, the

The Piper Came to Our Town

horsemen pursued the opposite direction; and when the piper either attempted to alight or expostulate with his friend Tom, he found both his limbs and tongue equally incapable of motion. They halted at the fort of Doon, near the river Araglin, where rose a stately building, the brilliant lights of which put to shame the lustre of the stars and the clear full moon.

In the great hall appeared a splendid company of both sexes, listening to the music of the full orchestra, where sat musicians bearing instruments with which the piper was wholly unacquainted; and bards in white robes, whose long beards flowed across their tall harps. An elderly man, bearing a long white wand, announced "Daniel O'Leary, the Duhallow Piper," and immediately three distinct rounds of cheering rose from the crowded assembly, till the fairy castle shook to the sound.

When the applause had subsided, a beautiful lady rose from her seat, and snatching a certain stringed instrument, sang to the music of its chords the following strain, addressed to the astounded piper:

Thy welcome, O'Leary, be joyous and high,
As this dwelling of fairy can echo reply,
The clarseach and crotal and loud bara-boo
Shall sound not a note till we've music from you.

The bara-boo's wildness is meet for the fray,
The crotal's soft mildness for festival gay,
The clarseach is meeter for bower and hall;
But thy chanter sounds sweeter, far sweeter than all.

When thy fingers are flying the chanter along,
And the keys are replying in wildness of song;
The bagpipes are speaking such magical strain,
As minstrels are seeking to rival in vain.

Shall bards of this dwelling admire each sweet tune,
As thy war-notes are swelling that erst were their own;

Shall beauties of brightness, and chieftains of might,
To thy brisk lay of lightness dance lightly tonight?

O'er harper and poet we'll place thy high seat;
O'Leary, we owe it to piper so sweet;
And fairies are braiding (such favorite art thou),
Fresh laurel unfading, to circle thy brow.

Thy welcome, O'Leary, be joyous and high,
As the dwelling of fairy can echo reply;
The clarseach and crotal and loud bara-boo
Shall sound not a note till we've music from you.

Then a seat that glittered like a throne was prepared for the delighted O'Leary, and a band of beautiful damsels, with laughing blue eyes, placed a garland of shining laurel 'round his head. The other performers were completely mute during the rest of the night. Fair ladies poured out the red wine and pressed the entranced piper to quaff the inspiring beverage. Every tune elicited fresh applause; and when the dancing ended the lords and ladies all declared that their hearts bounded lighter and their feet beat truer time to O'Leary's music than ever before.

At length, oppressed with wine, and intoxicated with the incense of applause, the piper sunk into profound repose. When he awoke in the morning he found himself reclining at the same bush to whose shelter he had retired to let the horsemen pass; the pipes were yoked and his left hand still grasped the chanter.

He at first conceived that the scenes of the preceding night, which began to assume a definite shape in his memory, were but the dream of imagination, heated by music, whiskey-punch and his conversation with Nancy Walsh; until he found the unfading wreath yet circling his brow. This wreath of laurel he had preserved and still exhibits as his fairy meed of musical excellence.

Such was the adventure of Daniel O'Leary; and the traveler from whose account of it we have liberally availed ourselves concludes: "Many are the opinions afloat concerning the truth of this narrative, but let skeptics examine, as I have done, this curious wreath of laurel, and consider its complicated braiding, and the piper's unimpeachable veracity in all other respects, before they presume to try this singular story by the test of their philosophy."

RORY OGE, THE KILLALOE PIPER

While speculating as to the probable site of the palace of Brian Boru at Kincora, and calling up in her fancy a long array of "chiefs and ladies bright," listening to the harp of the old minstrel, Mrs. S. C. Hall, who traveled extensively in Ireland early in the second quarter of the nineteenth century, tells in her writings how she was startled by the tones of the Irish bagpipes coming from Killaloe, nearly a mile distant.

It was a fair day in that ancient town, and after walking along with a gathering crowd she entered a tent from which the music proceeded and was introduced to the piper, familiarly known as Rory Oge.

"We found him," she says, "very chatty and communicative, as we have found others of his class, and mourning over 'ould times,' as pathetically as did his great prototype, Mac Liag, over the downfall of Kincora. He was particularly wrathful upon two or three points—the decay of mountain stills, the decline of dancing, the departure of all spirit out of the hearts of 'the boys,' and above all the introduction of brass bands." The amiable traveler found him so interesting and entertaining that she has immortalized him in her works.

"Rory Oge" or Young Rory, as he was always called, was as enthusiastic and yet knowing a piper as ever "blew music out of an empty bag." He was a large portly man with a bald high brow, framed in a quantity of greyish flaxen hair; his nose had a peculiar twist and his mouth was full of ready laughter.

Though blind from birth, he always jested about this infirmity, and he was in great request all over the country, being even a better piper than his father, Red Rory. The latter never attempted other than the old established Irish tunes, while Rory Oge the son, who had visited Dublin and once heard Catalani sing, assumed the airs of a connoisseur and extolled his country's music in a scientific way.

When he played some of the heart-moving Irish planxties, at the commencement of the movement he would endeavor to look grave and dignified; but before he was half through, his entire face expanded with merriment, and he would give "a whoop" with voice and fingers as it was concluded that manifested his genuine enthusiasm. Once in his life he had visited Dublin, expressly for the purpose of hearing Catalani, and when he was in the mood, to hear the recital of his interview with the "Queen of Song" was a source of much pleasure to his audience.

"You see," he would commence, "I thought it was my duty to hear what sort of a voice she had; and on my way to the great city, in the cool of the evening, I sat myself and my little boy by the side of two strames—the 'Meeting of the Waters' they call it—and it wasn't long till a thrush began to sing in a rowan tree on the opposite bank, and then another, and then a blackbird would give his tally-ho! Of a whistle high and above all the rest, and so they went on singing for ever so long. Then two or three would stop, and one great songster would have it all his own way for a while, and then when they would all start together a great flood of bird music would gush out again.

"In the midst of it all the little *gorsoon* fell asleep, and I felt the tears come down my face just within thinking of the beautiful music the Almighty puts into the throats of them fluttering birds, and wondering if the furrin' lady could bate the thrush in the rowan tree.

"In the afternoon of the next day, I was in Dublin, but not a bit of her was to tune up, till the night after; so I had to hould my patience another day. Why, God bless ye, the Dublineers were going just as mad about her singing as they are now about them nasty, braying brass bands, that has no more of the rale music in 'em than a drove of donkeys.

"Well dears, I'll not be thinking of 'em now putting me past my patience, only just come to the furriner, and more's the pity

The Piper Came to Our Town

she was one; so as I said, thinking as I was a born musicianer, and all my family for hundreds of years before me, I thought for the honor of the country I'd call upon her, for in troth I was just fairly ashamed of the fellows that were around her, from all I heard, giving her no iday of the rale music, only playing night after night at the theatre 'St. Patrick's Day,' as if there was ne'er another saint in the calendar, nor e'er another tune in the counthry.

"Well. I got my pipes claned, and my little guide boy a bran, new shoot of clothes, and, to be sure, meself was in the first fashion; and the lace ruffles round my wrists, that my father wore when he rattled the 'Connachtman's Rambles' to the House of Commons there in College Green, and so I sent up my card, and, by the same token. It was on the back of the ten o' diamonds I had it wrote; I knew the card by the ten punches of a nail Jimmy Bulger put in it, for I always had great divarshun with the cards, through the invention of Jimmy's—rest his soul—giving me eyes, as I may say, in the tips of my fingers; and I got the man to write on it 'Rory Oge, the piper of all Ireland and His Majesty, would be proud to *insense* Madame Catherlany into the beauties of Irish music.' Ye see, the honor of ould Ireland's melodies put heart into me, and I just went upstairs as bould as a rint agent, and before she could say a word I recited four varses of my own poethry that I composed on her.

"Oh, bedad! Girls, you may wink and laugh; but I'll tell you what—that's what she didn't do, but she welcomed me in her broken English and was as kind as a born Irish. 'Oh! Mr. Rori Ogeri, I'm so glad to see you,' and a whole lot more nate compliments she paid me, and asked me to play her an Irish jig.

"So, before commencing, I just said a few words, by the way, to let her see that I wasn't a mere bog-throtting piper at all, but wan that could play anything from Handel to Peter Purcell, or any of the Parley voos; and, betwixt and be-tween them all, there isn't a better air in any of their roratoryes than a march my own father played one day that restored an ould colonel officer to the use of his limbs—there was the power of music for you; and maybe she didn't think so, and maybe she wasn't delighted!

The Piper Came to Our Town   35

"Well, though I was consated enough to be proud at introjuic-ing to her my own family's music, *'twas the music of my countary my heart bate to tache her*; and so on afther a while I led on from wan fine ould ancient air to another—the glorious melodies of Ireland. Oh, but the wonder of the Irish music—do you see me now—is that its sweetness is never feeble, and its strength is nev-er rude; it's just a holy and wonderful thing, like the songs of the birds.

"Ah, then, jewel, Oge! maybe she didn't drink them down. 'Stop!' she'd say, and then she'd tune them over, every note as clear and pure as the silver bell the fairies (God bless us) do be ringing of a midsummer night under the green hills; and then she'd say, 'Play another,' and in the midst of it all would have my little guide into the room and trated us like a queen (and that's what she was) to fine ould wine. With that she says, 'Now you've played for me, and I'll sing for you,' and—she—did—sing! And now you'll think this hard to believe, but it's true—*she put me out of consate with the pipes!* She did, bedad! And it was as good as a week before I could bring myself to tatther a note out of 'em, though I left myself a beggar going to hear her sing."

In concluding her sketch, Mrs. Hall adds: "We left Rory in de-spair at the state of national music, and full of dread that, owing to the heresy of brass bands, he would be the last of the pipers."

REMMY CARROLL, THE FERMOY PIPER

Strange, is it not, that nearly all the pipers who have found a place in Irish literature hailed from the southern provinces. Perhaps they possessed other qualifications of an attractive nature which gained for them more attention than persons of this class in other parts of Ireland.

Such, at least, was the case with Remmy Carroll of Fermoy, whose "father before him" was a piper. Standing six feet two in his vamps, a perfect Adonis in shape and beauty, he could outwalk, outrun, and outleap any man in the parish or barony, or the next barony to it for that matter. No wonder such a man, having the additional charm of being a splendid performer on the plaintive pipes, was such a favorite among the fair colleens of Clongibbons, and, regardless of the shabby attire, could cut out at pleasure farmers' sons and thriving shopkeepers. Shelton Mackenzie tells us that "Carroll's performance could almost excite the very chairs, tables, and three-legged stools to dance." Like a true minstrel of the olden time, he was an independent citizen of the world, without a permanent abode, for every door was open to him, from Teddy Mulcahy's humble *bohaun* to Bartley O'Mahony's two-story slated house on a three-hundred-acre farm on the banks of the Blackwater.

His daughter, Mary, was an Irish beauty and no mistake—dark hair, fair skin, and violet eyes, and an heiress at that, having been left 500 pounds by a maiden aunt. With all her "fortune" and good fortune, she had neither pride nor conceit, although being the greatest matrimonial catch in the country. Of course, Remmy Carroll, like all the young men, loved her, but knew enough to "suffer in silence."

One Sunday, while returning from Mass, Mary and her cousin took the route along the river and across the fields on their way home. In attempting to jump across a small, deep stream, Mary was precipitated into the water. It was just the piper's luck to he near enough to hear the scream as she fell, to save her from drowning.

Mackenzie devotes pages of "fine writing" to the details of this incident and its resulting emotions, upon which our theme will not permit us to dwell, except to state that from that day the current of Remmy's life seemed changed.

In many respects he was above the generality of his class, for he had a tolerably good education, and not without a certain manly grace of manner. It must be understood that he was still a professional piper, but it was noticeable that his newly acquired habits of economy enabled him to dress quite tastily—in fact, to appear as a regular country beau.

"It is not now I'd be waiting to thank you, man alive," said Mr. O'Mahony to him, one Sunday after Mass, "but Mary never let me know the danger she'd been in till this blessed morning, when her cousin, Nancy Doyle, told me about the ins and outs of the accident. But I do thank you, Remmy, and 'twill go hard with me if I can't find a better way of showing it than by words, which are only breath as one may say."

Then the rich farmer familiarly slapped the piper on the back and insisted that he should accompany them and have dinner.

Everyone knows what effect walking home with Mary had on Remmy's smoldering love, and his frequent visits thereafter to see the "man of the house" never even roused a suspicion in the latter's mind that there could be anything but formal friendship and gratitude between two socially so far apart.

How to reward the piper for his heroic act in saving the rich man's daughter was a problem which O'Mahony solved by announcing that Mary should learn music and appointing Remmy to instruct her. But as he could play only upon one instrument, and that hardly suitable for a young lady, upon due consideration, the father decided to become the musical pupil himself.

At his age his progress was naturally slow, but that didn't matter as long as a legitimate way had been found to put money in Remmy Carroll's pocket, for that worthy would not take it under any other condition.

However, if the pupil did not make good use of his time the teacher did, and before the end of the first quarter Mary had half confessed to her own heart with what aptitude she had taken lessons in the art of love.

Nancey Doyle, her cousin, enjoyed the flirtation as being "fine fun," but it came to a climax one day as they were walking in the meadows.

Poor Remmy declared his love, not with any hope of its being reciprocated, but because he had to tell it or burst. Being unable to endure hopeless love any longer, he told her he was going away. With fine, ambiguous phrases, Mary endeavored to convey the idea that the case was not so hopeless, but, overpowered as her lover was by emotion, he did not seem to understand.

"It's no use trying to banish you from my mind. I've put a

penance on myself for daring to think of you, and it's all no use. I try to forget you in the day, but I can't, and when I sleep at night you come into my dreams. Wherever I am, or whatever I do, you are beside me with a kind, sweet smile. It's all no use—I will go for a soldier, and if I am killed in battle, as I hope I may be, they will find your name written on my heart."

Who can blame Mary if she confessed her love under the circumstances. "Remmy! Dear Remmy, you must not leave me. If you go my heart goes with you, for I like you better than the richest lord in the land with his own weight of gold and jewels on his back."

We will leave to the imagination of the reader how they parted. Mary went home, her heart torn by conflicting emotions, while Remmy Carroll returned to Fermoy, not knowing whether he stood on his head or his heels.

After resting at his friend Pat Minahan's house for a few hours they set out about dusk for a farmer's house, where there was to be a wedding that night, for Remmy and his pipes were almost as indispensable as the priest or the bridegroom.

His mind was so preoccupied with the thought of Mary O'Mahony, the pearl of his heart, that Minahan's stories of fairies and enchantment fell on dead ears until they reached their destination, where the celebrated piper received the very warmest of welcome.

To describe the "carryings on" at an Irish wedding would be superfluous to the majority of Irish readers, for the festivities are as much alike as one pea is the twin of another—"a sort of mirthful madness," as Mackenzie terms it.

In compliance with the custom at all wedding feasts, where whiskey-punch was as plenty as tea at an old maids' evening party, our piper drank a man's share of the beverage of which it is boasted that "there's not a headache in a hogshead of it." Yet he had not exceeded the bounds of sobriety. His friend Minahan, who had indulged a little more freely, insisted on going home to Fermoy, although he had been proffered a bed in the barn.

So Carroll and Minahan left the house together, linked arm in arm, for the latter was a little wobbly in his gait. The next day Minahan was found lying fast asleep with a soft stone for a pillow, near the footpath at the base of Corran Thierna, but of the piper there was not a trace, as if the earth had swallowed him. His pipes were found on the ground near Minahan, and uninjured.

The whole district was alarmed, for the piper was very popular, so in the course of a few days Father Tom Barry, the parish priest, called on Minahan for an explanation.

Grief for the loss of his friend so affected the latter that, between that and the potheen he drank to drown it, Father Barry found him in bed. "Oh! Them fairies! Them thieves of fairies!" was all the reply he could make to his reverence when half aroused.

When he came to his senses, of which he had never a superfluity, and after he limbered his tongue with a "wetting," he spun out a most weird and wonderful yarn about what befel himself and the piper when they came to the fairy ring on their way home.

Fairy music filled their ears, and a thousand lights suddenly glanced up from the said ring, like an illumination for some great victory. "Then came a thousand dawney fairies, who began dancing jigs as if there were springs in their heels, intermingling backwards and forwards, to and fro. At last one of them came out of the ring and, making a leg and a bow as genteel as ould Lynch, the dancing master, said: "Mr. Carroll," says he. "Would you be so kind and condescending and so darn'd disobliging as to oblige us and disoblige yerself and to give us a 'chune'? 'Tis we'd like to foot it a step or two, for," says he, "'tis ourselves have often heard of your beautiful playing." Then the little mite of a fairy fixed his eyes upon Remmy, and that I mightn't ever if they didn't shine in his head like two coals of red fire, or a cat's eye under a blanket.

Remmy told them modest enough that he was no player for the likes of them. Ah! they'd take no excuse, so, with their fine soothering talk and fixing a stone for a seat for him, he struck up 'Garryowen' in a way that would lift you off the floor. The way St. Vitus danced wasn't a patch to the way they went at it.

"There was nothing slack or deficient about the way Remmy let them have it, until one of the 'faymale' fairies slipped undher his elbow and suggested, 'Maybe, Mr. Carroll, you'd be dhry?' The piper, seeing she was 'purty,' smiled sweetly, but the question being repeated, he said he had been to a wedding and wasn't particularly dry, but he'd drink a good husband to her, soon, and many of them."

Well, to make a long story short, Remmy drank out of the little morsel of a glass she gave him, something that was stronger than holy water. She kissed the glass as he took it, and as he appeared so much refreshed, Minahan, thinking some of the same cordial would be good for his own complaint, he called out to Remmy to save a drop for him. The words were hardly out of his mouth when—whoop! Away they vanished, just as Remmy threw his pipes to Minahan by way of a keepsake and dashed down through the earth with the rest of them!

"But, Minahan," said Father Barry, "you certainly don't mean to pass off this wild story for fact?"

"But I do, your Reverence," said Minahan, rather testily, "and that's all I know about it."

Slowly but surely does the tide of time carry year after year into the eternity of the past. Bartley O'Mahony met with a fatal accident; his daughter Mary, yet unmarried, mourned for her mysteriously missing sweetheart, whose disappearance for six long years was a subject for much speculation and the theme of many a tale.

Yet he returned, brawny and bearded, knowing nothing of what transpired during his absence, and when he disclosed his identity his loyal and constant Mary received him with open arms and, as in the conventional love stories, they were married and lived happy ever after.

The true story of Remmy Carroll's disappearance was scarcely less thrilling than Minahan's supernatural tragedy.

It may be remembered that Remmy had acted as escort to Minahan on their return from that wedding at which the piper had officiated professionally. He had found much difficulty in piloting his companion along the high road from Rathcormac to Fermoy, and when they reached the mountain path Minahan insisted on throwing himself upon the heathy sward, where in a few minutes he was fast asleep. The piper, having seen him safe that far, didn't like to leave him, so he sat down beside him. After a time he, too, very naturally became drowsy, and as a precaution against accident he placed his pipes on the ground some little distance from them and lay down to sleep.

His slumber must have been profound, for on awaking, to his amazement he found himself on a baggage cart, with his head reposing on the lap of a soldier's wife for a pillow, while her husband occupied the driver's seat. No explanations were offered until they reached Glanmire, when the sergeant in charge informed him that he was a duly enlisted recruit in his majesty's service. His remonstrance was useless, for there was the "shilling" in his pocket, the silent but indisputable evidence that he had, all unbeknown to himself, become attached to the military service of "His Most Gracious Majesty, King George the Third." His remonstrances, denials, and appeals to the officer in command were all in vain, and, as he was carefully watched, escape was impossible.

After the regiment had embarked for the Peninsula, the fierce sergeant told as a good joke how he came to be enlisted.

While the regiment was passing along by the foot of the mountain (Corran Thierna), one of the officers who rode above the highway had noticed Remmy and Minahan asleep, and, marking what an able soldier the former would make, he was picked up bodily and placed in one of the baggage carts without awakening him.

It was long before an opportunity was given him to write, and being afraid that a letter addressed to his heart's idol, Mary O'Mahony, might fall into other hands and betray him, he did write to Minahan. The letter, if ever posted, never reached its destination, and thus for more than six years he was lost to the world at home.

What can't be cured must be endured, so our hero philosophically followed the trade of a soldier, conducted himself admirably, and was promoted to the rank of sergeant.

He lost an arm at the battle of Waterloo. With a respectable pension and a handsome gratuity for the loss of a limb, and what he had already saved up, Remmy Carroll returned to Ireland in good circumstances.

Bronzed and bewhiskered as he was, Mary did not penetrate the disguise, but she was loyal to his memory and had remained unmarried. The wedding followed in due course, and was sure enough a notable event at Carrigbrack, but Minahan's character for "truth and veracity" fell very much into disrepute thereafter in that part of the country.

THE SILENT PIPER

By a peculiar combination of circumstances not a piper or fiddler was available to play at the wedding of Mickey Donovan's daughter Biddy to Morty Maguire, away back in the year 1840, when by unexpected good luck, who should come along but a strange piper. He was a thin, spare, plaintive-looking, under-sized man, much bent by age or sorrow, or perhaps by a mingling of both. Being stone blind, he was led by a pretty, sunny-haired little maiden not yet in her teens.

His opportune appearance was hailed with delight by every member of the family, busy though they were preparing for the next day's nuptials, for he carried his welcome with him in the bagpipes under his arm.

"What can you play sir, if you plase?" questioned the pretty bride-to-be.

"'Haste to the Wedding,' or whatever you plase, miss," answered the little girl, half shyly.

"And why can't your father answer for himself?" inquired Biddy.

"If you plase, miss, it's a vow that's on him for a raison he has," replied the child, "and so I'm his speech as well as his eyes myself, miss."

"Oh, indeed!" "Poor man!" "See that now!" "A vow!" "Oh musha, but sin is a shockin' thing!" were the exclamations that followed.

"'Tis no sin of his own," observed the child; "only one he took upon himself, for one he loved."

The Irish are a very inquisitive people, and though Biddy had too much delicacy to urge the little girl to betray the piper's secret, the other members of the family were in no way restrained by any such consideration.

After the strangers had been warmed and fed, and every one who could dance had "taken a turn on the flure" to the melodious piping of the old man, artful questioning elicited from the child the information that the blind piper was her father, and that her mother when dying "left a vow on him." He had never spoken since. She did not care to say where they came from, and she could not tell where they were going to.

Kelly, the local piper whose instrument was out of commission, was obliged to confess on the wedding day that he wasn't fit to "hould a candle" to the "silent piper," and everybody declared they had never heard such beautiful music. One or two very old people hinted that all was not right, for they had heard pipers and pipers in their youth, but such music as the newcomer played had never been heard before.

The fame of the "silent piper" reached the houses of the gentry; all who heard him were charmed by his wonderful performance. Liberal offers were made to the blind man if he would settle in the neighborhood; a cottage and garden would be given him, and all his wants supplied.

In reply he only shook his head and sighed and the little maid with tears in her eyes observed: "We have but a short time to stop now, as father seldom stayed more than a week in any one place."

"Obligations" or "vows" were not uncommon among the Irish peasantry, but no one had ever heard of an instance like this. The little daughter by her winning ways had achieved as much popularity as her father, and there were very few who had not bestowed some gift or token of remembrance on both. However, the best of friends must part, so to signalize his leaving the old man played "O'Carolan's Lament" until he drew tears from the eyes of many of his audience.

Many years afterwards, while visiting the ancient and picturesque town of Kinsale, Mrs. S. C. Hall, from whose writings this story has been abstracted, heard the sound of a bagpipe, and followed it to be nearer the player. Had a spectre risen from the earth she could not have been more astonished, for there after a lapse of nearly twenty years sat the "silent piper" with the very same blooming child at his knee!

He played again the bold brave notes of "Brian Boru's March," and the women stamped their feet to the tune and hoisted their little ones in the air, and when he finished they gave so loud a cheer that it animated the old man to an encore of the national march, and all the time the famous author was deeply pondering at the marvel of finding the "silent piper" of Bannow, County Wexford, after a lapse of so many years in the town of Kinsale, County of Cork.

"Eh dear!" said the old man when questioned; "do I mind Bannow? To be sure I do; God be with it!"

"And you?" to the girl half doubtingly.

"I never was there nor in the City of Cork either, ma'am," she answered.

While the well-remembered bead necklace glittered in the sun, and the very same blue ribbon seemed to confine her fair hair.

"Ah. My dear lady," pleasantly interposed the old piper, "that was her mother, God bless ye! Her own mother, my daughter Kathleen, who is the mother of a family now," and while the good lady was smiling at her own absurdity the original Kathleen made her appearanee—a stout gleeful-looking woman with a mild bland laugh, but with twins in her arms, and twins at her side.

Certainly the realities of life sadly upset the imagination. How our mental pictures are shattered.

"Sure I have all the little keepsakes and tokens I got still," she said with pride; "and the tears do be coming in my eyes when I think of them, and the penance my poor father took on himself that time; he's half childish now and would be so entirely but for the music, and that is what mainly keeps up his interest in life."

A SATANIC PIPER

A curious tradition prevalent in a little village in Somersetshire, England, respecting the origin of four groups of stones which formed when complete two circles, serves to remind us that

Ireland and the Scottish Highlands had no monopoly of legendary tales in which pipers were the leading characters.

Many hundred years ago on a Saturday evening (so the story runs) a newly married couple, with their relatives and friends, met on the spot now covered by those ruins to celebrate their nuptials. Here they feasted and danced right merrily until the bell in the church tower tolled the hour of midnight, when the piper—a pious man—refused to play any longer. This was much against the inclinations of the guests, and so exasperated the bride, who was fond of dancing, that she swore an oath that she would not be balked of her enjoyment by a beggarly piper, but would find a substitute if she went to the lower regions to get one.

She had scarcely uttered the words when a venerable old man with a long beard made his appearance, and having listened to their request, proffered his services, which were gladly accepted.

The suave old gentleman, who was no other than the arch-fiend himself, took the seat vacated by the godly piper, buckled on his burnished instrument, and commenced playing a slow and solemn air. This wasn't the music his audience wanted—far from it—and they were by no means timid about telling him so. Accordingly he changed the tune into one more lively and rapid.

The company now began to dance, but soon found themselves whirling round the demon piper so fast and furiously that they were more than anxious to rest. But when they attempted to retire they found to their consternation that they were revolving with increased velocity round their diabolical musician, who had resumed his original shape. Their cries for mercy were unheeded until the first glimmering of day warned the fiend that he must depart.

With such rapidity had they moved that the gay and sportive assembly were now reduced to a ghastly troop of skeletons. "I leave you," said the fiend, "a monument of my power and your wickedness to the end of time." He then promptly vanished. The villagers on rising in the morning found the meadows strewn with large pieces of stone and the pious piper lying under a hedge, half dead with fright, having been a witness to the whole transaction.

The Piper Came to Our Town

The Irish Bagpiper

One day in the leafy month of June an angler wandered by a brook-side in a deep glen. Tall rocks and trees rose at either side, and tinkling silver threads of water ran down to the bigger stream in many places. The spot was lonely but not savage. It was full noon, and so warm that after a while the fisherman left off work and found a moss patch to rest on. And as he rested he heard that native concert which is ever going on in due season and weather amongst birds, and bees, and grasshoppers, and other creatures that rejoice in the summer for the sun in their own language. But of a sudden, in the midst of the soft croon of pigeons, the occasional flute-call of that wonderful musician with the golden bill, the deep and always as it were distant bassoon of the flower-robber, there came the queerest, quaintest tangle of sounds, scarcely more rhythmical or measured than the performances of doves, honey-gatherers, gnats, or river.

It mingled with them quite naturally. And when a wind swept for a moment down the glen, and the trees whispered to each other the singular tune, or as it seemed the odds and ends of a hundred tunes, combined also with *that* effect as if the breeze-sigh and leaf-flutter were part of the symphony. And the fisherman gets up to go in search of the accomplished elf who has come out of the hollow hills to practice airs he must play for his gay companions under the stars by the haunted rath. And he follows the brook path, and the music becoming louder he knows he is approaching the source of it. And this he observed, that as the tune (and it now began to have a distinct or half-distinct outline) was less dispersed by distance, it was not altogether so magical in character, though yet strangely and sweetly becoming the scene over which it was rambling.

And finally the angler is drawn by the ear to the very feet of his Orpheus. Think you he saw the ghost of an ancient harper in white, seated like a gray friar on a gray stone, or the fairy fiddler above mentioned, or beheld a figure blowing into a sheaf of reeds with the power of the great god Pan, or any other beautiful demon or sprite born of a poet's fancy, or of an artist's dream, or say of any ink bottle (talk of your ocean being kind to us for casting up one Venus, how many as beautiful divinities have emerged from our oceans of ink?)—think you he saw—but this reads like a passage of the *Critic*—what he did see was an old man playing the Irish pipes, with a dog for an audience, unless a goat is to be counted who has stopped munching bush-tops for a moment on the other side of the brook.

An old man, obviously blind, dressed poorly but not raggedly. His hat, to be sure, has seen better days; but considered as a ruin, it has a picturesque appearance. And the angler quietly intended to listen to the music without announcing himself, but the dog would not permit such a liberty to be taken with his master's property, and so he barked a sentence of barks as who would say, Master, here is a scurvy fellow who has his ear cocked for the purpose of stealing our tunes; whereupon the pipes left off with a kind of snarl that had nothing at all pastoral or idyllic about it.

The piper was on his way to a wedding and a christening in the neighbouring village. He was rehearsing for his performances. It was not difficult to set him going again. Well, he was not Pan, Orpheus, Mars, Bacchus, Apollo, or Virorum. He was a common piper, and yet the music he made amongst the rocks and trees sounded still far more sympathetically than I imagine the music of the best trained orchestra would. I, for I was the eavesdropping angler, dislodged the goat and sat thus some distance from the player. The tunes are all supposed to be cheerful. "The Foxhunter's Jig," listen to that for merriment! The tallyho, tallyho! quite plain on the tenor notes, the hound-music and its echoes, the call of the horn, the death of the *modereen ruadh*, and through it always the dance itself, to which these mimetic references are only asides, garnish. I encore the "The Foxhunter's Jig," and my ancient bard pumps away at it again with such renewed spirit that if he doesn't move the rocks he makes them speak, for they repeat many of the

The Piper Came to Our Town

wild cadences, the dog gives an awakened bark of approval, and from behind a doomed shrub peers the big astonished eyes of the goat with his beard and horns, the very picture of a faun!

And so again we join the chase, and do double shuffle in the jig besides, and then an end of the foxhunter business, and we start with "Nora Creina." Nora Creina is not as successful a hit. The musician employs his chanter with bad effect. "Oh my Nora Creina, dear," and similar affectionate passages, are not well translated into orchestral form when the phrase is expressed in hoarse asthmatic tones. You perceive I am candid as to the bagpipes, and no enthusiast about them when the measure of their function and capacity has been exceeded.

—by W. Barry, from *The Casquet of Literature*, edited by Charles Gibbon, 1873.

—❖—

Let ither poets rave and rant,
How fiddles can the saul enchant,
How harps and organs lift the sanct
To heaven aboon;
For me, my lugs I winna grant
To sic like din.

The swelling horn, and sounding drum.
Yield pleasing notes nae doubt to some;
And chiels wha at pianos thrum,
Think nought's sae braw;
But Scotland's skirling bagpipe's bum
Is worth them a'.
From "The Bagpipes" by William Murdoch

The Piper of Mucklebrowst

About a century since, in the last "rugging and riving days" of Scotland, before the modern march of intellect had so completely routed the wonderful arts of magic and witchcraft as to leave neither witch nor conjuror in all the broad lands of Britain, there lived a noted fellow called Rory Blare, who filled the office of town-piper to the prosperous fishing port of Mucklebrowst. He always affirmed his family to be of high antiquity, and as he was disclaimed by the Blairs of that Ilk, and the Blairs of Balthayock, and the Blairs of Lethendie, and the Blairs of Overdurdy, and, in short, by all the other Blairs, he set up at once to be the head of the Blares of Bletherit and Skirlawa', which have furnished Scotland with pipers ever since it was a country.

In this course of his life Rory had performed the various parts of fisherman, sailor, soldier, and pedlar, none of which professions are peculiarly likely to teach a man temperance; and having procured his discharge in consequence of a wound in his head, which carried away a small fraction of his brain-pan, about the sober age of fifty-seven he settled down into a roistering and carousing town-piper.

As he had a good deal of those rambling, mischief-loving, satirical characters, called in Scotland *hallen-shakers* and *blether-skytes*, and his strangest tricks were played, and his fun was ever the most furious when the malt was over the meal, all who knew him declared that "he certainly had a bee in his bonnet, puir man! ever sin' he gat that sair paik on his pow in the wars." Rory himself, however, was wont to assert that "he was as gude a man as ever;" which, perhaps, might be true in one sense, as he never was very celebrated for either his prudence or his sobriety.

So much for his person and character; and for his talents as a piper, he could most merrily "blaw up the chanter," as the old song says, with some skill and "richt gude will," untired, even through

The Piper Came to Our Town

a long night of active dancing and loud carousal; which, with his mirth and hold demeanour, made him a special favourite through-out Mucklebrowst and its vicinity. Without at all underrating his own knowledge of music, he was fond of attributing some part of his popularity to his instrument, which, he was accustomed to relate, had been found in one of the holy wells of St. Fillan, in Perthshire; thereby inheriting a finer tone and easier breath than any mere mortal pipes could ever boast of, beside the power of resisting all kinds of glamour or witchcraft. The truth of this was never rightly known, though it was whispered that, if the pipes *had* belonged even to St. Fillan himself, Rory Blare had employed them so differently, that if they ever possessed any virtue it had long since departed.

As the worthy town-piper was always ready to be foremost in any kind of sport, or to bestow his counsel in any case of court-ship, marriage, or witchcraft, which occupied the gossips—that is to say, all the inhabitants of Mucklebrowst—he was everywhere welcome. But, though he distributed his patronage pretty equally, he appeared to be most merry, and to make himself most at home, at the Maggie Lauder's Head, a little public kept by one Bauldie Quech, whose jovial and careless disposition matched exactly with his own. They would frequently sit till "the sma' hours," driv-ing away time by glass after glass, rant after rant, and song af-ter song, until the decease of Katie Quech, Bauldie's contentious spouse; when, though all expected to see him take a younger and more agreeable partner, and had even settled who it was to be, he suddenly sank into a dismal and melancholy mood, under the influence of which he drank twice as much as before, though he never laughed at all.

Rory Blare, however, did not desert his old companion; for in-deed the warmth of his friendship very frequently led him to sit piping and drinking with him throughout the whole night; and one dark and windy evening in autumn they were thus engaged, with a single sedate-looking stranger habited in pale gray, who had come in about night-fall.

"Hont, tout, man!" exclaimed Rory, finding that even St.

Fillan's blessed pipes had no effect upon his host, "ye're unco hard to please, I trow; and yet yere lugs used to ken whan they heard gude music: but I daur say the deil's cussen his cloak owre ye, as King Jamie said o' his bairn. Ye'll no think now, honest frien'" continued he, addressing himself to the guest, "that the gudeman was anee ane o' the merriest men o' Mucklebrowst, though ever sin' Luckie Quech died he's no had a word for a dog, let alone a blythe lad or a bonnie lassie."

"Let him look for another Luckie, then, and the sooner the better," answered the stranger, "take heart, man, there's as good fish in the sea as ever came out of it."

"And that's true too, though the deil himsel' spak it," rejoined the piper. "I'm thinkin', Bauldie, that I'll hae to play 'Fy, let us a' to the bridal,' before ye yet. And wha shall it be, gudeman? Wha shall it be? For ye ken there's a hantle o' bonnie lassies in Mucklebrowst, to speak naething o' them o' Leven, or the limmers o' Largo. But ye'll look to the tocher, billie, and see that the lass has a quick lug for the music, and a light fit for the dance."

"They may hae what they will for me," at length answered the host, with a deep sigh, "and they may be as bonnie as they will for me; but they can nane o' them be either less or mair to me."

"Think again, friend," said the guest, "and you will think better of it, for I've often known as broken a ship come to land. What say ye now to Sibbie Carloups, of Gouks-haven, with golden hair on her head, and gold coin in her pouch; I promise you now, that she'd be the girl for me."

"She was no that unsonsie a lassie, but, she was nae muckle better than wud, or a witch, when she leevet there," returned the piper, "but that's fu' twenty years agone, for she suddenly gaed awa' and no ane kenned where, though folk said she went mad, or was carried awa' to be the deil's jo, some gate about Forfar or Glammie."

"It's a' true!" exclaimed Bouldie Quech, in voice of great distress, "it's an ower true tale, as I ken fu' weel, and fu' sadly, though I didna think to hae tauld what I ken o't to ony ane but the minister: but Rory, ye're a fearless and lang headed chiel at a hard pass, and as ever ye did gude to a puir body at their wits' ende, ye maun e'en help me now."

"Say awa' then wi' yere story, neebor," returned the piper, "and if it be in the skeel o' man, and I dinna stand by you, may the deil burst the bag o' my pipes, and split the drone and chanter!"

"Weel, weel," answered the host, with more composure, "I'm no misdoubting ye, though I trow it's past your art: but at ony rate it will gie some ease to my mind; so I'll e'en mak a clean breast, and tell ye a' about it. About twenty years back, as ye said, Sibbie Carloups was the wale o' the lassies o' this coast, though a wild tawpie, and I was no then a bad looking lad mysel'; and as we fore-gathered thegither mair than anee, I e'en tell'd her my mind, and she listened to me, and sae at last we brak a saxpence in twa for a true love token; but frae that hour I saw her nae mair, for the vera next time I went to Gouks-haven, she was departed."

"And did you no follow her, man?" demanded Rory Blare, "ye suld hae followed her ower land and lea till ye met again; I'se war-rant she wadna hae 'scaped me like the blink o' a sunbeam."

"I did follow her," said Bauldie Quech, "and that for mony a lang and weary mile, and speir'd at every ane that I earn nigh, but I ne'er saw her again; and sae, when I heard some auld carlines say that belike the witches had carried her awa', I e'en gied her up; for naebody can find out what they dinna like to show. Weel, I cam back to Mucklebrowst, and years passed awa', and I thought nae mair o' the matter; and at last I weddit Luckie Links, o' St. Mo-nan's; and then, as ye ken, she went to a better warl', and left me to get through this as I could. Weel, man, wad ye think it, she had-na been gane a week or mair, when an auld, ill fa'ard, grewsome, gyre carline cam up to the door ae muckle dark and windy even, when I was my lane, and called me her ain gudeman, and said she was Sibbie Carloups, come to claim my promise o' marriage! 'And where hae ye been a' this time, Sibbie?' says I, when I could speak for wonder, and some little o' fear; 'Troth, lad,' said she, 'I canna just tell ye where I hae been; a frien' o' mine has taken me to see the warl', and made me gay rich, but ye see I dinna forget auld acquaintance; here's the half o' the saxpence we brak, and as yere first jo's dead, we'll e'en be marryit when ye will.' 'Marry thee!' thought I, 'I'll suner see thee linkit to a tar-barrel!' But I was fain to speak her fairly, and so I askit her to come ben: but she tauld me that there was sic a bush at my door that there was nae getting by it. 'Oh, ho! Luckie!' thought I again, 'it's the rowan-tree branch, is it? There it shall hing then for me.' So I drew me back a wee, and then said bauldly, 'I'll e'en tell ye the truth, cummer; folk say ye've been made a witch of, and I'm judging it's true; but for byganes' sake ye'll get nae harm frae me, only tak up yere pipes and begone; but first gie me back my siller, for I'll hae naething mair to do wi' yon.' 'Aha, billic,' then said the auld carline, 'there are twa words to that; if ye're fause and ungratefu', that's yere ain fault; but while I've the broken saxpence I can weel hinder yere marrying ony body without my leave, and may be do a little mair; sae think o' that, and be wiser in yere passion.' To mak the least o' a lang story, at last she sae put up my bluid that I rushed out o' the house to lay baud on her,—when, fizz, she was gane like the whup o' a whirlwin', and the night was too dark to see whilk way the deil had carried her! And after a' I haena done wi' the auld jaud, for in the darkest and wildest nights she comes rattling at the window-bole, and crying out that she's my ain jo, and has our broken saxpence; but when I gae out I can tak haud o' nought, and see naething but a flisk o' her fiery eyes as she mounts up owre the house-rigging into the clouds on the nightmare. And now ye hae heard my story, I hae nae mair to say, than that I wad gae half my gudes to onybody wha wad get me back the half saxpence, and send Sibbie Carloups to be brunt at the Witches' Howe at Forfar."

"Baith o' whilk I wad do blithely," said the piper, "gin ye could tell me where I could find the witch-carline; for I wadna think muckle o' meeting her and her haill clanjamfray wi' St. Fillan's pipes; I trow I'd gae them sic music as they ne'er dancit to before."

"Waes me! then," exclaimed Bauldie Quech in reply, "for there's nae finding a witch against her will; sae there's no help for me in this warld."

"But there may be some in another," said the stranger-guest, "and I think I can show it, if your piper-friend be only as stout and fearless as he seems; I promise you that his success is certain, and that the only danger will be in shrinking back when the work is begun."

"Deil doubt me then," said Rory, "there's my thumb on't: and ye ken I'm no vera sune daunted."

"Then," answered the stranger, "the sooner you set out the better, since you may have a long journey before you; so mount my horse, for he knows the way you're going; ride out of the town towards Glammis, and you will meet a number of persons, with whom Sibbie Carloups will certainly be. Ask them for Gossip Paddock; and say to her, that you come from Melchior the comptroller, who commands her to give up Bauldie Quech's token; but take heed that you have no other intercourse with them, and, above all, that you bring nothing else away with you."

With these instructions and his blessed pipes Rory Blare departed, followed by the anxious hopes and good wishes of the host. He was nothing dismayed at the cheerless appearance of the night, which was overclouded; whilst a violent storm of wind roared round him, seeming as if it raged purposely to impede his progress. He rode on at a rapid pace; but the way looked wilder and more lonely than usual, no person appearing of whom he might make his mystic inquiries. The features, too, of that well-known road seemed altogether altered, since the piper missed the little towns and change-houses with which he knew it to be studded; though he failed not to recognize, with increased terror, the spots which had been rendered famous by any fearful circumstances. At length, however, he entered a deep and spacious glen, covered with dark heather, which was wholly unknown to him; so that he was now assured that he had missed his way altogether.

As the wind still continued to blow furiously, and the rain to fall with violence between the gusts, Rory Blare was rejoiced to see the dim outline of a building appear in the glen before him, one part of which was glowing with lights, and resounding with the loudest notes of merriment. He made up to it, if it were only in the hope of getting some information of his way and a temporary shelter; and arriving at a little stone portal, which was half open, beneath the lighted chambers, he rang, and knocked, and shouted for some time, without procuring any reply. Alighting from the stranger's horse, therefore, and fastening him to the door, he went in and ascended a flight of narrow winding stairs, which terminated in a suite of state-chambers, decorated in the style, however, of three centuries before. The room which he first entered was richly illuminated, and in the centre appeared a table, round which several tall powerful men were seated, playing at cards. They were all habited in the most costly and antique dresses; for there were pall and velvet, steel armour and two-handed swords, and robes of ermine and minever. They swore and stamped at each other, raged and shouted in the most fearful manner, as they won or lost the broad gold pieces which lay on the table before them; but the most furious of all was one old hard-featured baron who sat at the head of the chamber, distinguished from the rest by an immensely long beard. He lost much and repeatedly, tore the cards and dashed his clenched hands passionately on the board, then called for wine, and again engaged in the game, swearing in the wildest manner that he would play on till doomsday.

The terrific features of this scene made even the piper desirous of exchanging it for the stormy night and dark glen without; but upon looking round for the door by which he entered, he found that it had closed, and was covered by hangings similar to the rest of the room, so that it could nowhere be seen. Whilst he was gazing about him for some other passage, he was accosted by the long-bearded nobleman, who demanded of him in a thundering tone what he wanted, and who sent him there. Rory felt his blood rather chilled whilst he answered that he had missed his way to Glammis, on the road to which one Master Melchior the comptroller had sent him to inquire for Gossip Paddock, to recover a token from her.

"The fiend take Melchior the comptroller!" exclaimed the ancient baron, "he'll ruin the trade of us a', if he gae on at this rate. And what base carle are ye, whom he has sent on sic a fule's errand?"

"I'm Rory Blare, the town-piper o' Mucklebrowst, if it like your honour," was the reply; "I hae the blessed pipes o' St. Fillan wi' me, and I'll gie ye ane of the Saunt's ain sangs by which he drave awa' the deil on the chanter, an ye wad like to listen till it."

There was something in this proposal not very pleasing to the long-bearded baron, since he ground his teeth and grinned fearfully upon the piper, and roared out fiercely to Nickie Deilstyke to take the canting dog down to the revel in the court-yard, and show him where Cummer Paddock hung her curch whilst she danced. Rory Blare followed the servitor through several winding passages, into what seemed to him a churchyard, surrounded by a ruined cloister, and part of an ancient chapel, with a running stream forming the lower boundary. Both the building itself, which appeared to be illuminated, and the grassy cemetery, were crowded with a host of females, young and old, fair and foul, dancing furiously to the sound of the deepest and shrillest pipes Rory had ever heard. The tune in general was a loud and continued rant, held on in the same clamorous key, though it often swelled suddenly into a positive howl of wild merriment, increased by the shouts and shrieks of enraptured dancers: which, however, sounded in the piper's ears more like cries of pain than those hearty halloos of pleasure which distinguish the native dances of Scotland.

Rory's guide stopped at a whin-bush beside a fallen column, and pointing to a dark-coloured hood hanging upon it, directed the piper to seize it, and when the owner came up to make his own terms for its restoration, since she would never he able to quit that place without it. He had scarcely laid hold of it, and thrust it into his bosom under the Saint's pipes, when a woman, bent almost double, and with features nearly resembling those of a toad, came up to him, and in a whining flattering voice entreated him to give it back; adding, that she would give him many gifts, and specially teach him to play as never piper played before. All her entreaties, however, availing nothing until she produced Bauldie Quech's troth-pledge, the witch in a rage flung the broken coin upon the ground, exclaiming, "There, you suspicious tyke, will ye no gie me my curch now?"

"Let's see if a' be right first, Luckie," answered the invincible piper, "all's not gowd that glitters, ye ken;" and having taken the pledge from the ground, and satisfied himself that there was no deception, he thrust it into his breast, and approaching the running stream, drew out the witch's hood and hurled it in, saying, "There, cummer, as the gudeman at Mucklebrowst wants nae mair o' yere visits, we'll e'en tak awa' yere power o' making them!"

The witch gave a wild shriek as she saw her magic curch sink down, with a dark flush of fire, in a place where she had no power to follow it; knowing also that the loss of it involved her own instant destruction. A loud shout of exultation immediately arose from the wizard crowd, which came pouring down and whirled away the unfortunate Sibbie Carloups, after which she was never more seen on earth.

The music then changed to a brisk and sprightly tune, still frequently played in Scotland, though formerly condemned as an unhallowed spring—called "Whistle o'er the lave o't." This was a strain in which Rory was considered to have extraordinary skill; and being animated by the well-known notes, and elated by his recent victory, he at once forgot his hazardous situation and the saintly character of his pipes; and leaping up on the broken pillar he cried out. "Lilt awa'! cummers, lilt awa'! yon birkie blaws the chanter unco weel; but I'd play that spring wi' Auld Clootie himsel, sae here goes till ye;" but with the very first notes the bag of his instrument suddenly burst, and the pipes split from top to bottom! "Deil's in't!" exclaimed the alarmed Rory Blare, "if there's no an end o' the blessed pipes o' St. Fillan! God hae us in his keeping! What are we to do now?"—but scarcely had he uttered the holy name when the whole scene was swept off in a howling whirlwind, and he saw no more till he found himself, at daybreak, lying with the broken pipes and the love-token, under the ancient walls of Glammis Castle, upwards of thirty miles distant from Mucklebrowst.

Having made the best of his way back to Bauldie Quech, he found him quite another man, and joyfully preparing for his marriage with Janet Blythegilpie, of the East Green, it being already known that Sibbie Carloups had been carried away in a fearful storm of wind, on Hallowe'en, at midnight; which the piper's story and the production of the broken sixpence were supposed entirely to confirm. It was never very clearly made out how long Rory Blare had been gone, where he had been, or who was the stranger by whose advice be went; for, whilst the piper affirmed that he was absent but a single night, all Mucklebrowst declared that his office had been vacant for a week; and that he was certainly away at the fearful season of Hallowe'en. As to the second point, it was agreed that he had wandered to Forfar or Glammis Castle, or perhaps had a drunken vision in the ruins of Restennet Priory. The howling of the wind through the arches, and his imagination, familiar with the superstition of those places, might have supplied the witches, music, and revelry; together with the revelation of that secret chamber, wherein Alexander, surnamed Beardie, third Earl of Crawford, is supposed to be playing at cards until the day of judgment. And lastly, the person by whose counsel he went on the journey was very generally considered to be a famous white wizard, or benevolent magician, who used his art to counteract the powers of darkness.

Bauldie Quech became a person of consequence in Mucklebrowst, being made treasurer; and his name yet lives in its traditions for having kept the municipal moneys in a manner worthy of the most primitive ages of the world. His depositories were nothing less than two large jack-boots, which hung beside his fireplace; into one of which he threw all sums received, and into the other all his vouchers for payments. At the end of the year both were emptied and a balance struck, though it is reported that, as there was some deficiency in the debtor-boot, it was thought more prudent to transfer the trust to other hands; notwithstanding which, the ex-treasurer always asserted that it was the best way possible of keeping the accounts, since every one in his dwelling was of indubitable honesty, and "it saved a wheen hantle o' perplexing buiks and skarts o' writing." The good town also gave Rory Blare a new stand of pipes, by the first maker of his time, but they were never thought to be equal to those of St. Fillan; and to his dying hour he could never be prevailed upon to play the 'witching tune of "Whistle o'er the lave o't."

—by Richard Thomson, from *The Casquet of Literature*, edited by Charles Gibbon, 1873.

—❖—

Again I hear you piping, for I know the tune so well, —
You rouse the heart to wander and be free,
Tho' where you learned your music,
not the God of song can tell,
For you pipe the open highway and the sea.
O piper, lightly footing, lightly piping on your way,
Tho' your music thrills and pierces far and near,
I tell you you had better pipe to someone else to-day,
For you cannot pipe my fancy from my dear.

You sound the note of travel
through the hamlet and the town;
You would lure the holy angels from on high;
And not a man can hear you, but he throws the hammer down
And is off to see the countries ere he die.
But now no more I wander, now unchanging here I stay;
By my love, you find me safely sitting here:
And pipe you ne'er so sweetly, till you pipe the hills away,
You can never pipe my fancy from my dear.
From "The Piper" by Robert Louis Stevenson

The Highland Piper

A Highland piper shot through both his feet,
  Lay on the ground in agonising pain;
The cry was raised, 'The Highlanders retreat;
  They run, they fly, they rally not again!'
The piper heard, and, rising on his arm,
  Clutched to his heart the pipes he loved so well,
And blew a blast—a dirge-like shrill alarm,
  That quickly changed to the all-jubilant swell
Of 'Tullochgorum.' Swift as lightning flash,
  Or fire in stubble, the tumultuous sound
Thrilled through the clansmen's hearts, and with a dash
  Of unreflecting valour, at one bound
They turned upon their hot-pursuing foes,
  And faced them with one wild tempestuous cheer
That almost drowned the music as it rose
  Defiant o'er the field, loud, long, and clear!
Scotland was in it, and the days of old
  When, to the well-remembered pibrochs of their sires,
They danced the exultant reel on hillsides cold,
  Or warmed their hearts with patriotic fires.
The startled enemy, in sudden dread,
  Staggered and paused, then, pale with terror, fled;
The clansmen followed—hurling shout on shout —
  In martial madness on the hopeless rout.
'Twas but five minutes from the set of sun,
  And ere it sank the victory was won!
Glory and honour, all that men can crave,
  Be thine, o piper, bravest of the brave!

—by Charles Mackay, from *The Highland Bagpipe*,
edited by William Laird Manson, 1901.
Originally titled "The Piper."

Ould Murphy the Piper

Ould Murphy the Piper lay on his deathbed,
To his only son Tim, the last words he said,
'My eyes they grow dim, and my bosom grows could,
But ye'll get all I have, Tim, when I slip my hould,
Ye'll get all I have, boy, when I slip my hould.

'There's three cows and three pigs, and three acres of land,
And this house shall be yours, Tim, as long as 'twill stand;
All my fortune is threescore bright guineas of gould,
An ye'll get all I have, Tim, when I slip my hould,
Ye'll get all I have, Tim, when I slip my hould.

'Go fetch me my pipes, Tim, till I play my last tune,
For death is coming, he'll be here very soon;
Those pipes I have played on, ne'er let them be sould,
If you sell all I have, Tim, when I slip my hould.'

Then ould Murphy the Piper, wid the last breath he drew,
He played on his pipes like an Irishman true,
He played up the anthem of Green Erin so bould—
Then calmly he lay down and so slipt his hould!
Then gently he lay down and slipt his last hould.

—by Alex A. Ritchie, from *The Highland Bagpipe,*
edited by William Laird Manson, 1901.

The Piper Came to Our Town

Black Chanter of Chattan

According to one story, the Feadan Dubh, *The Black Chanter, fell
from Heaven in the Battle of the Clans (also known as the Battle of
the North Inch), 1396. This poem was dedicated by the author to the
Battle of Culloden, the final battle in the 1745 Jacobite Uprising.*

Black Chanter of Chattan now hushed and exhausted,
    Thy music was lost with the power of the Gael;
The dread inspiration Mac Pherson had boasted
    For ever expired in Drummossie's sad wail.

On old St. Johnstone's dark meadow of slaughter
    Thy cadences buried the piper's last breath;
The vanquished escaped amid Tay's rolling water,
    The conqueror's pibroch was silenced by death.

That piper is nameless, and lost in like manner
    The tribes are forgotten of mighty Clan Quhele;
While Chattan that bears the hill-cat on his banner,
    No time can extinguish, no ruin assail.

From the hand of a cloud-cleaving bard thou wert given
    To lips that embraced thee till nerveless and dead;
Since then never idly Mac Pherson hath striven,
    Nor trust in his fortune been shaken by dread.

O mouth-piece of conquest! who heard thee and trembled!
    Who followed thy call, and despaired of the fight?
Availed not that foemen before thee dissembled,
    For quenched was their ardour and nerveless their might.

The blast of thy pibroch, the plaint of thy streamer,
    Lent hope to each spirit and strength to each arm;

While the Saxon confronting was scared like the dreamer
    Whose sleep is of peril, of grief, and alarm.

Led on by thy promise, what chieftain e'er sallied
    Nor proved in the venture how just was thy vaunt?
At the spell of thy summons exultingly rallied
    The faltering pulse of dispirited Grant.

Forerunner of victory! Why didst thou tarry?
    Thy voice on Drummossie an empire had changed;
We then had not seen our last efforts miscarry,
    The Stuart had triumphed, the Gael been avenged.

Ah, fatal Drummossie—sad field of the flying!
    The Gathering sank in the hopeless Lament;
What pibroch could stanch the wide wounds of the dying?
    What magic rekindle the fire that was spent?

Proud music, by shame or dishonour ne'er daunted,
    By murmur of orphan, by widowed despair,
The fall of thy country thy spell disenchanted,
    With the last of the Stuarts it vanished in air!

Yet rouse thee from slumber, Black Chanter of Chattan,
    Send forth a strong blast of defiance once more;
On the flesh of thy children the vulture doth fatten,
    And sodden with blood are the sands of Lahore.

As fierce as the tiger that prowls in their forest,
    Those sons of the Orient leap to the plain;
But the blade striketh vainly wherever thou wanest,
    Black Chanter of Chattan bestir thee again!

—by Mrs. Ogilve, from *The Highland Bagpipe*,
edited by William Laird Manson, 1901.

The Piper Came to Our Town

Pibroch o' Donuil Dhu

*This is a very ancient pibroch belonging to Clan MacDonald, and
refers to the expedition of Donald Balloch, who, in 1431, launched
from the Isles with a considerable force, invaded Lochaber, and
at Inverlochy defeated and put to flight the Earls of Mar and
Caithness, though at the head of an army superior to his own. The
words of the set, theme, or melody to which the pipe variations are
applied, run thus in Gaelic, with the translation in English:*

> *Piobaireachd Dhonuil Dhuidh, piobaireachd Dhonuil;*
> *Piobaireachd Dhonuil Dhuidh, piobaireachd Dhonuil;*
> *Piobaireachd Dhonuil Dhuidh, piobaireachd Dhonuil;*
> *Piob agus bratach air faiche Inverlochi.*
> *The pipe-summons of Donald the Black,*
> *The pipe-summons of Donald the Black,*
> *The war-pipe and the pennon*
> *are on the gathering-place at Inverlochy.*

Pibroch of Donuil Dhu,
Pibroch of Donuil,
Wake thy wild voice anew,
Summon Clan-Conuil.
Come away, come away,
Hark to the summons!
Come in your war array,
Gentles and commons.

Come from deep glen, and
From mountain so rocky,
The war-pipe and pennon
Are at Inverlocky.
Come every hill-plaid, and
True heart that wears one,

Come every steel blade, and
Strong hand that bears one.

Leave untended the herd,
The flock without shelter;
Leave the corpse uninterr'd,
The bride at the altar;
Leave the deer, leave the steer,
Leave nets and barges:
Come with your fighting gear,
Broadswords and targes.

Come as winds come, when
Forests are rended,
Come as the waves come, when
Navies are stranded:
Faster come, faster come,
Faster and faster,
Chief, vassal, page and groom,
Tenant and master.

Fast they come, fast they come;
See how they gather!
Wide waves the eagle plume,
Blended with heather.
Cast your plaids, draw your blades,
Forward each man set!
Pibroch of Donuil Dhu,
Knell for the onset!

—by Sir Walter Scott, from *The Poetical Words of Sir Walter Scott,*
        edited by Joseph H. Francis and Samuel H. Parker, 1845.

The Piper Came to Our Town

When Bagpipes
Held No Charm

An amusing episode recorded of the Peninsular War[1] seems to prove that even the charms of our beautiful national bagpipes fail to soothe savage breasts!

It happened that, while one of the Highland regiments was marching across a desolate part of Spain, one of the pipers for some inexplicable reason found himself separated from his comrades. Halting on a lonely plain, he sat down to eat his breakfast, when, to his horror, he saw wolves approaching. When they came very near he flung them all the food he had with him, fully conscious, however, that this meagre meal would not stay their advance for many seconds.

With the calmness of desperation he then said: "As ye've had the meat ye'll ha'e the music," and he began to blow up his chanter. No sooner did his unwelcome guests hear the first skirl of the pipes than they turned in wild terror and fled as fast as their long legs would carry them.

"De'il ha'e ye!" said the piper; "had I thocht ye were sac fond o' the music ye wad ha'e gotten it afore meat instead o' after!"

Then hungrily he went his way, not forgetting from time to time to blow a blast so wild and shrill as might effectually scare any prowling foes.

—From *Our Dumb Animals,* 1892.

---

1. Also known as the Spanish War of Independence. It was a contest between France and the allied powers of Spain, the United Kingdom, and Portugal for control of the Iberian Peninsula during the Napoleonic Wars. The war began when French armies invaded Portugal in 1807 and Spain in 1808 and lasted until the defeat of Napoleon in 1814.

Purcel the Piper

Jack Purcel was a good-humored, ruddy-faced young man, compact and vigorous. He was spirited and generous, and as brave as a lion. He could wrestle, kick foot-ball, jump, or hurl better than any boy of his size in the parish of Mullinahone. But the pride of Mullinahone, the mountain maid of Tipperary, was the charming Grace Donnelly, the flower of Slieve-na-Mon. Jack Purcel loved Grace, and, of course, as a natural consequence, Grace returned the compliment.

Now, Phil Donnelly, the father of the fair young Grace, was acknowledged to be the greatest piper in the four provinces. Phil, though a generous, warmhearted man, had one fault, if fault it can be called, and that was vanity—vanity in his musical prowess— and to such a pitch did he carry it, that one evening, at a merry-making near the cross-roads, he registered a vow that no boy in the whole county would ever get his consent to marry Grace.

"No," said he, "she'll go single all her life, barrin' that whoever would marry her can prove himself a better piper than her father."

"That seals my fate," said poor Jack Purcel, "for I know no more about music than I do o' the Greek language."

"Och, Grace, jewel," said Jack to his colleen, one bright morning in June; "what is to be done, darlin', at all, at all? Your father's vow the other night was like a death knell to my hopes."

"Jack, *acushla*, don't break down that way—all's not lost yet. Can't ye go into practice for a year or two, an' who knows but in the coorse o' time ye'd be able to bate my father."

"Bate yer father, is it? No, Grace, not if I kep' practisin' from this till Tib's Eve. The dickens in it, for music, it has brought two faithful hearts to a purty pass."

"Do ye know what I was thinkin', Jack?"

"What was it, Grace?"

"Of coorse, ye know the spot called the Fairy Cave."

"I do; in the side of Slieve-na-Mon, about three miles from this. Well, what about the Fairy Cave, machree?"

"I'm towld, Jack, that the sweetest sounds can be heard comin' out of it on a quiet night."

"That's true enough, jewel, if we're to believe what we hear."

"An' 'tis said, if any one has the courage to enter it they get such a knowledge o' music that no human skill can aquil."

"Grace, darlin'," said Jack, "I had my mind med up on emigratin' to Ameriky, but your cheerful words make a new man o' me. So, instead o' crossin' the Atlantic, I'll visit the Fairy Cave to-night."

"To-night?"

"Yis, darlin', I'll make hay while the sun shines."

"But if the good people should make a prisoner o' ye in the mountains for life, what's to become o' me?"

"Don't be afeerd, Grace, darlin'; before you are three days owlder you'll see me again, and even if I don't happen to find the gift o' music, my heart, like your own, will still be in the right place, *mavourneen.*"

After a few mutual promises they parted.

On the evening of that day Jack Purcel set out for the mountains of Slieve-na-Mon, having previously provided himself with a torch and taking with him for company his friend Billy Donovan. The hour was now a little past twilight; the road to the fairy cave was wild and desolate; on each side of them were a variety of lonely hikes and abrupt precipices; the sun had just gone down. In about an hour, however, after much difficulty, they succeeded in reaching the Fairy Cave. The entrance was thickly overgrown with briars and bushes.

At length, having cleared away every obstacle, they soon discovered an opening in the mystic cave, and after lighting the torch Jack Parcel and his friend proceeded on their way, often stopping to admire the beauty of the landscape that presented itself to their view as they advanced. In the far distance rose the outlines of a hill whose green and sloping base melted into the moonlit bosom of a smooth lake.

"Begorra, Billy," whispered Jack to his friend, "Killarney

couldn't howld a candle-to this purty spot."

Sometimes they were compelled to creep on their hands and knees through the narrowest passes until they arrived at the margin of the lake.

Beside the lake was a green fairy ring, into which as Purcel inadvertently stepped, he was struck to the earth and instantly deprived of all consciousness.

He was awakened by the sounds of soft music, and opening his eyes beheld surrounding him a large company of little people playing on musical instruments, who, the moment they saw that he was awake, desired him to follow them, and touching him with their wands they immediately flew across the lake, Jack having become as aerial as any of them in their midst, and alighted on an island which, they informed him, was named "The Isle of Music." Through this happy island flowed a river of such crystalline clearness that Purcel could plainly distinguish the gleaming of the precious gems which studded its bed. Flocks of birds varying in beauty skimming through the air joined their gushes of melody to the rapturous combination of sounds pervading the island; not a dog barked nor a cow lowed but in the purest harmony.

Purcel was then conducted by the fairies into the presence of a venerable man with a long white beard, descending to his chest. This was the Bard of the Isle of Music.

The bard held his court on a beautiful elevation covered with the softest moss of never-fading green.

"Mortal, whence come you?" demanded the bard, as he looked with a stern eye upon the trembling Jack Purcel.

"From Mullinahone, your mighty hardship," replied Jack.

"What is your name?"

"Misther John Purcel, at your royal sarvice."

"And why are you here, trespassing on our dominions?"

"I kem here, your majesty, to see if I could bony a loan o' the gift o' music before I begin to learn the bagpipes."

"O, you wish to become a piper?"

"Yes, your hardship, the best in Ireland, if it's plazin' to ye."

"Know you not," said the bard, "that the gift of music seldom bestows happiness on its possessor?"

"I know, your majesty, that the same gift would make me the happiest man alive, for it's then I'd be able to marry the colleen o' my heart, Grace Donnelly."

Jack then told the bard the whole of his sorrows, and how his love for Grace had occasioned his visit to the Fairy Cave. The bard was touched and highly gratified by poor Purcel's devotion to his betrothed.

"Well, Jack," he exclaimed, "you shall have your wish." So saying he ordered one of his attendants to pick him a bagpipe off the nearest tree, and then, commanding silence, played that sweetest and most sorrowful of all the melodies, the Irish air of "Shuil Agra," with such exquisite pathos that the tears ran in torrents down the tender visage of Jack Purcel; the dying cadences were softly echoed by the soughing of the trees and the melodious whispers of the flowers.

"By the powers o' delight," cried Purcel, "if I was the owner o' them pipes I'd feel prouder than a king this minit. I only wish they wor mine—it's then I'd bring the joy to the sorrowful hearts o' the poor."

"Jack Purcel," said the bard solemnly, "your request is granted. You came here with a pure motive for the sake of the girl you love, and from this hour," he added, handing Jack the bagpipe, "you are the most celebrated piper in green Erin."

Jack, on being requested to favor the court with a sample of his newly-acquired skill, bowed, and taking the instrument into his hands, felt such a flood of inspiration rushing upon him that the buoyancy thereof nearly lifted him off his feet.

He then began, and, considering that it was his debut, and that his audience was formed of first-rate judges, he displayed considerable confidence and self-assurance. To his ecstatic delight he found himself complete master of the instrument. The piece he performed was the spirit-stirring strain of the "Blackbird," and the shrill chanter, as it rang across the hike, elicited tumultuous applause; after which Jack, in gratitude, prostrated himself at the foot of the emerald throne to tender his warm acknowledgment for his invaluable gift, when suddenly the whole scene disappeared, and he found himself, not in a fairy ring, where the good people had discovered him, but carefully deposited near the entrance to the Fairy Cave. The first terrestrial sound that greeted his ear was the voice of his friend, Billy Donovan.

"Arrah, man alive, d'ye mane to sleep yer sivin sinses away?"

Jack essayed to answer, but could not; he had only time to feel that the inspired pipe was still under his arm, before relapsing again into insensibility; in this state he was borne to his mother's cabin, where he lay in a profound slumber for three days, at the expiration of which he awoke, and, seizing the enchanted pipes, burst forth into such strains of music that in less than an hour brought the whole parish of Mullinahone to listen to him, and so powerful was the impression he made that young and old pronounced him the best piper in the universe. Even Phil Donnelly himself acknowledged his superiority. And, if we are to believe our fireside chronicler, Grace Donnelly eventually became the wife of the finest piper in Ireland.

—❖—

*Twelve clansmen
and one bagpipe
make a rebellion.*
Sir Walter Scott

The Piper Came to Our Town

The Piper

Loud he piped for them to dance—
Oh, the gay retreat, advance,
　　Like surging waves that lean and lift
To know the red star's glance!
　　And their bare brown feet's refrain
　　Was like patter of the rain
　　　　That thrills in May time through the green
　　Where cloistered birds are fain.

Gay the piper played the while grinned he craftily,
"Oh, rare and ripe for this I pipe, pay ye must," quoth he.

Oh, the dancers' eyes were bright
As a flame in middle night,
　　For shrill he piped the lure of life,
The daring of delight.
　　And they tripped it to and fro
　　As the light-foot fairies go
　　　　That circle on the greensward
　　When a crescent moon dips low.

Fast the piper played the while grinned he craftily,
"For this my tune or late or soon, pay ye must," quoth he.

Oh, the piper's notes were sweet
As a rose in noontide heat,
　　And Love was like the pulse of flame
That through his measure beat,
　　Oh, of love his pipings were
　　Till the air was all astir
　　　　With fragrance of his music
　　Spilled as spikenard and as myrrh.

Soft the piper piped the while grinned he craftily,
"For this my best and loveliest pay ye must" quoth he.

But what time the twilight died
Oh, he flung his pipes aside,
   And "Sweethearts, now comes reckoning!"
Grim Time the piper cried.
   "Give me guerdon for my pains,
   Give me payment for my strains,
     Now yield me for your pleasuring
   The price my piping gains."

"Nay, but wherewith may we pay?" Grinned he craftily,
"Youth of you and truth of you and joy of you," quoth he.

Oh, the shrinking forms and bent,
Oh, the weary feet that went
   Through dust of all regretting
From the place of merriment!
   And again the piper blew
   For another madder crew
     In silver of the moonlight
   And the shimmer of the dew.

Gay the piper played the while grinned he craftily,
"Yea, good sooth, I pipe for youth and take my pay," quoth he.

                  —from *The Joy o' Life and Other Poems*
                  by Theodosia Pickering Garrison, 1909.

—❖—

Some men there are love not a gaping pig;
some, that are mad if they behold a cat;
and others, when the bagpipe sings...cannot contain their urine.
William Shakespeare

                The Piper Came to Our Town

The Wonderful Tune

Maurice Connor was the king, and that's no small word, of all the pipers in Munster. He could play jig and planxty without end, and Ollistrum's March, and the Eagle's Whistle, and the Hen's Concert, and odd tunes of every sort and kind. But he knew one, far more surprising than the rest, which had in it the power to set every thing dead or alive dancing.

In what way he learned it is beyond my knowledge, for he was mighty cautious about telling how he came by so wonderful a tune. At the very first note of that tune, the brogues began shaking upon the feet of all who heard it—old or young it mattered not—just as if their brogues had the ague; then the feet began going—going—going from under them, and at last up and away with them, dancing like mad! Whisking here, there, and everywhere, like a straw in a storm—there was no halting while the music lasted!

Not a fair, nor a wedding, nor a patron in the seven parishes round, was counted worth the speaking of with out "blind Maurice and his pipes." His mother, poor woman, used to lead him about from one place to another, just like a dog.

Down through Iveragh—a place that ought to be proud of itself for 'tis Daniel O'Connell's country—Maurice Connor and his mother were taking their rounds. Beyond all other places Iveragh is the place for stormy coasts and steep mountains: as proper a spot it is as any in Ireland to get yourself drowned, or your neck broken on the land, should you prefer that. But, notwithstanding, in Ballinskellig Bay there is a neat bit of ground, well fitted for diversion, and down from it, towards the water, is a clean smooth piece of strand—the dead image of a calm summer's sea on a moonlight night, with just the curl of the small waves upon it.

Here it was that Maurice's music had brought from all parts a great gathering of the young men and the young women— *O the darlints!*—for 'twas not every day the strand of Trafraska was stirred up by the voice of a bagpipe. The dance began; and as pretty a rinkafadda it was as ever was danced. "Brave music," said everybody, "and well done," when Maurice stopped.

"More power to your elbow, Maurice, and a fair wind in the bellows," cried Paddy Dorman, a hump-backed dancing-master, who was there to keep order. "'Tis a pity," said he, "if we'd let the piper run dry after such music; 'twould be a disgrace to Iveragh, that didn't come on it since the week of the three Sundays." So, as well became him, for he was always a decent man, says he: "Did you drink, piper?"

"I will, sir," says Maurice, answering the question on the safe side, for you never yet knew piper or schoolmaster who refused his drink.

"What will you drink, Maurice?" says Paddy.

"I'm no ways particular," says Maurice; "I drink anything, and give God thanks, barring *raw* water. But if 'tis all the same to you, Mister Dorman, may be you wouldn't lend me the loan of a glass of whiskey."

"I've no glass, Maurice," said Paddy; "I've only the bottle."

"Let that be no hindrance," answered Maurice; "my mouth just holds a glass to the drop; often I've tried it, sure."

So Paddy Dorman trusted him with the bottle—more fool was he; and, to his cost, he found that though Maurice's mouth might not hold more than the glass at one time, yet, owing to the hole in his throat, it took many a filling.

"That was no bad whiskey neither," says Maurice, handing back the empty bottle.

"By the holy frost, then!" says Paddy, "'tis but could comfort there's in that bottle now; and 'tis your word we must take for the strength of the whiskey, for you've left us no sample to judge by;" and to be sure Maurice had not.

Now I need not tell any gentleman or lady with common understanding, that if he or she was to drink an honest bottle of whiskey at one pull, it is not at all the same thing as drinking a bottle of water; and in the whole course of my life, I never knew more than five men who could do so without being overtaken by the liquor. Of these Maurice Connor was not one, though he had a stiff head enough of his own—he was fairly tipsy. Don't think I blame him for it; 'tis often a good man's case; but true is the word that says, "when liquor's in sense is out;" and puff, at a breath, before you could say "Lord, save us!" out he blasted his wonderful tune.

'Twas really then beyond all belief or telling the dancing. Maurice himself could not keep quiet; staggering now on one leg, now on the other, and rolling about like a ship in a cross sea, trying to humour the tune. There was his mother too, moving her old bones as light as the youngest girl of them all; but her dancing, no, nor the dancing of all the rest, is not worthy the speaking about to the work that was going on down upon the strand. Every inch of it covered with all manner of fish jumping and plunging about to the music, and every moment more and more would tumble in out of the water, charmed by the wonderful tune. Crabs of monstrous size spun round and round on one claw with the nimbleness of a dancing-master, and twirled and tossed their other claws about like limbs that did not belong to them. It was a sight surprising to behold. But perhaps you may have heard of father Florence Conry, a Franciscan friar, and a great Irish poet; *bolg an dana*, as they used to call him—a wallet of poems. If you have not, he was as pleasant a man as one would wish to drink with of a hot summer's day; and he has rhymed out all about the dancing fishes so neatly, that it would be a thousand pities not to give you his verses; so here's my hand at an upset of them into English:

> *The big seals in motion,*
> *Like waves of the ocean*
> > *Or gouty feet prancing,*
> *Came heading the gay fish,*
> *Crabs, lobsters, and cray-fish,*
> > *Determined on dancing.*

> *The sweet sounds they follow'd,*
> *The gasping cod swallow'd;*

'T was wonderful, really!
And turbot and flounder,
'Mid fish that were rounder,
   Just caper'd as gaily.

John-dories came tripping;
Dull hake by their skipping
   To frisk it seem'd given;
Bright mackrel went springing,
like small rainbows winging
   Their flight up to heaven.

The whiting and haddock
Left salt water paddock
   This dance to be put in:
Where skate with flat faces
Edged out some odd plaices;
   But soles kept their footing.

Sprats and herrings in powers
Of silvery showers
   All number out-number'd.
And great ling so lengthy
Were there in such plenty
   The shore was encumber'd.

The scollop and oyster
Their two shells did roister,
   Like castanets fitting;
While limpets moved clearly,
And rocks very nearly
   With laughter were splitting.

Never was such an ullabulloo in this world, before or since; 'twas as if heaven and earth were coming together; and all out of Maurice Connor's wonderful tune!

The Piper Came to Our Town

In the height of all these doings, what should there be dancing among the outlandish set of fishes but a beautiful young woman —as beautiful as the dawn of day! She had a cocked hat upon her head; from under it her long green hair—just the colour of the sea—fell down behind, without hinderance to her dancing. Her teeth were like rows of pearl; her lips for all the world looked like red coral; and she had an elegant gown, as white as the foam of the wave, with little rows of purple and red sea weeds settled out upon it; for you never yet saw a lady, under the water or over the water, who had not a good notion of dressing herself out.

Up she danced at last to Maurice, who was flinging his feet from under him as fast as hops—for nothing in this world could keep still while that tune of his was going on—and says she to him, chanting it out with a voice as sweet as honey:

"I'm a lady of honour
Who live in the sea;
Come down, Maurice Connor,
And be married to me.

"Silver plates and gold dishes
You shall have, and shall be
The king of the fishes,
When you're married to me."

Drink was strong in Maurice's head, and out he chanted in return for her great civility. It is not every lady, may be, that would be after making such an offer to a blind piper; therefore 'twas only right in him to give her as good as she gave herself—so says Maurice,—

"I'm obliged to you, madam:
Off a gold dish or plate,
If a king, and I had 'em,
I could dine in great state.

With your own father's daughter
    I'd be sure to agree;
But to drink the salt water
    Wouldn't do so with me! "

The lady looked at him quite amazed, and swinging her head from side to side like a great scholar, "Well," says she, "Maurice, if you're not a poet, where is poetry to be found?"

In this way they kept on at it, framing high compliments; one answering the other, and their feet going with the music as fast as their tongues. All the fish kept dancing too: Maurice heard the clatter, and was afraid to stop playing lest it might be displeasing to the fish, and not knowing what so many of them may take it into their heads to do to him if they got vexed.

Well, the lady with the green hair kept on coaxing of Maurice with soft speeches, till at last she over persuaded him to promise to marry her, and be king over the fishes, great and small. Maurice was well fitted to be their king, if they wanted one that could make them dance; and he surely would drink, barring the salt water, with any fish of them all.

When Maurice's mother saw him, with that unnatural thing in the form of a green-haired lady as his guide, and he and she dancing down together so lovingly to the water's edge, through the thick of the fishes, she called out after him to stop and come back. "Oh then," says she, "as if I was not widow enough before, there he is going away from me to be married to that scaly woman. And who knows but 'tis grandmother I may be to a hake or a cod—Lord help and pity me, but 'tis a mighty unnatural thing. And may be 'tis boiling and eating my own grandchild I'll be, with a bit of salt butter, and I not knowing it! Oh Maurice, Maurice, if there's any love or nature left in you, come back to your own ould mother, who reared you like a decent Christian!"

Then the poor woman began to cry and ullagoane so finely that it would do any one good to hear her.

Maurice was not long getting to the rim of the water; there he kept playing and dancing on as if nothing was the matter, and

The Piper Came to Our Town

a great thundering wave coming in towards him, ready to swallow him up alive; but as he could not see it, he did not fear it. His mother it was who saw it plainly through the big tears that were rolling down her cheeks; and though she saw it, and her heart was aching as much as ever mother's heart ached for a son, she kept dancing, dancing, all the time for the bare life of her. Certain it was she could not help it, for Maurice never stopped playing that wonderful tune of his.

He only turned the bothered ear to the sound of his mother's voice, fearing it might put him out in his steps, and all the answer he made back was—"Whisht with you, mother—sure I'm going to be king over the fishes down in the sea, and for a token of luck, and a sign that I'm alive and well, I'll send you in, every twelvemonth on this day, a piece of burned wood to Trafraska." Maurice had not the power to say a word more, for the strange lady with the green hair seeing the wave just upon them, covered him up with herself in a thing like a cloak with a big hood to it, and the wave curling over twice as high as their heads, burst upon the strand, with a rush and a roar that might be heard as far as Cape Clear.

That day twelvemonth the piece of burned wood came ashore in Trafraska. It was a queer thing for Maurice to think of sending all the way from the bottom of the sea. A gown or a pair of shoes would have been something like a present for his poor mother; but he had said it, and he kept his word. The bit of burned wood regularly came ashore on the appointed day for as good, ay, and better than a hundred years. The day is now forgotten, and may be that is the reason why people say how Maurice Connor has stopped sending the luck-token to his mother. Poor woman, she did not live to get as much as one of them; for what through the loss of Maurice, and the fear of eating her own grandchildren, she died in three weeks after the dance—some say it was the fatigue that killed her, but whichever it was, Mrs. Connor was decently buried with her own people.

Seafaring men have often heard, off the coast of Kerry, on a still night, the sound of music coming up from the water; and some, who have had good ears, could plainly distinguish Maurice

Connor's voice singing these words to his pipes:
Beautiful shore, with thy spreading strand,
Thy crystal water, and diamond sand;
Never would I have parted from thee
But for the sake of my fair ladie.

—From *Fairy Legends and Traditions of the South of Ireland*
by Thomas Crofton Croker, 1882.

—❖—

What needs there be sae great a fraise
Wi' dringing, dull, Italian lays;
I wadna gie our ain strathspeys
For half a hunder score o' them;
They're dowf and dowie at the best,
Dowf and dowie, dowf and dowie,
Dowf and dowie at the best,
[Wi' a' their variorum;]
They're dowf and dowie at the best,
Their allegros an' a' the rest.
They canna please a Scottish taste
Compared with Tullochgorum.
From *The Highland Bagpipe*
by William Laird Manson, 1901.

The Pipes o' Gordon's Men

Home comes a lad with the bonnie hair,
And the kilted plaid that the hill-clans wear;
And you hear the mother say,
"Whear ha' ye ben, wee Laddie; whear ha' ye ben th' day?"
"O! I ha' ben wi' Gordon's men;
Dinna ye hear th' bagpipes play?
And I followed th' soldiers across the green,
And doon th' road ta Aberdeen.
And when I'm a man, my Mother,
And th' Hielanders parade,
I'll be marchin' there, wi' my Father's pipes,
And I'll wear th' red cockade."

Beneath the Soudan's sky ye ken the smoke,
As the clans reply when the tribesmen spoke.
Then the charge roars by!
The death-sweat clings to the kilted form that the stretcher brings,
And the iron-nerved surgeons say,
"Whear ha' ye ben, my Laddie; whear ha' ye ben th' day?"
"O, I ha' ben wi' Gordon's men;
Dinna ye hear th' bagpipes play?
And I piped th' clans from the river barge
Across the sands, and through the charge.
And I—skirled—th' pibroch—keen—an' high,
But th' pipes—ben broke—an' —my—lips—ben—dry."

Coronach

Upon the hill-side, high and steep,
Where rank on rank the soldiers sleep,—
Where the silent cannons beside the path,
Point the last forced-march that the soldier hath,—
Where the falling grave-grass has partly hid

The round-shot, heaped in a pyramid—
A white stone rises. Across its face
You can read the words that the chisels trace:
"Whear ha' ye ben, wee Laddie; whear ha' ye ben th' day?"
"O, I ha' ben wi' Gordon's men;
Dinna ye hear th' bagpipes play?"

—by J. Scott Glasgow, from *The Home Book of Verse: American and English 1580—1912,* selected and arranged by Burton Egbert Stevenson, 1915.

—❖—

The Concert Man's Ramble the piper did play,
When old folks and young kept dancing away;
But the music stopped short, for the bottle was dry,
And in under the table the piper did lie.
From the traditional song "The Old Country Party"

The Piper Came to Our Town

The Young Piper

There lived not long since, on the borders of the County Tipperary, a decent honest couple whose names were Mick Flanigan and Judy Muldoon. These poor people were blessed, as the saying is, with four children—all boys. Three of them were as fine, stout, healthy, good-looking children as ever the sun shone upon. It was enough to make any Irishman proud of the breed of his countrymen to see them about one o'clock on a fine summer's day, standing at their father's cabin door with their beautiful flaxen hair hanging in curls about their heads, and their cheeks like two rosy apples, and a big laughing potato smoking in their hands. A proud man was Mick of these fine children, and a proud woman, too, was Judy. Reason enough they had to be so. But it was far otherwise with the remaining one, which was the third eldest.

He was the most miserable, ugly, ill-conditioned brat that ever God put life into. He was so ill-thriven that he never was able to stand alone, or to leave his cradle. He had long, shaggy, matted curled hair, as black as the soot, and his face was of a greenish-yellow color. His eyes were like two burning coals and were forever moving in his head as if they had perpetual motion. Before he was a twelvemonth old he had a mouth full of great teeth and his hands were like claws. His legs were no thicker than the handle of a whip, and about as straight as a reaping hook. To make the matter worse, he had the appetite of a cormorant, and the whinge, and the yelp, and the screech, and the yowl was never out of his mouth.

The neighbors all suspected that he was something not right, particularly as it was observed when people, as they do in the country, got about the fire and began to talk of religion and good things. The brat, as he lay in the cradle his mother generously put near the fire place so that he might be snug, used to sit up in the middle of their talk and begin to bellow as if the Devil himself was in him. This, as I said, led the neighbors to think that all was not right, and there was a general consultation held one day about what would be best to do with him.

Some advised to put him out on the shovel, but Judy's pride was up at that. A pretty thing, indeed, that a child of hers should be put on a shovel and flung out on the dunghill like a dead kitten or a poisoned rat; no, no, she would not hear to that at all.

One old woman, who was considered very skilful and knowing in fairy matters, strongly recommended her to put the tongs in the fire and heat them red hot, and to take his nose in them. That would no doubt make him tell what he was and where he came from (for the general suspicion was that he had been changed by the Good People.) But Judy was too soft-hearted, and too fond of the imp, so she would not give in to this plan. Everyone said she was wrong, and maybe she was, but it's hard to blame a mother.

Well, some advised one thing, and some another, and at last one spoke of sending for the priest, a very holy and a very learned man. He would see to it. To this Judy of course had no objection, but one thing or other always prevented her doing so, and the up-shot of the business was that the priest never saw him.

Things went on in the old way for some time longer. The brat continued yelping and yowling, and eating more than his three brothers put together, and playing all sorts of unlucky tricks for he was mighty mischievously inclined.

That is, until it happened that one day Tim Carrol, the Blind Piper, called in while going on his rounds and sat down by the fire to have a bit of chat with the woman of the house. So after some time Tim, who was no churl of his music, yoked on the pipes and began to bellow away in high style. The instant he began the young fellow—who until this moment had been as still as a mouse—sat up in his cradle and began to grin and twist his ugly face, to swing about his long tawny arms, and to kick out his crooked legs. He showed every sign of taking great glee at the music. At last nothing would serve him but that he should get the pipes into his own hands. To humour him his mother asked Tim to lend them to the child for a minute. Tim, who was kind to children, readily consented. As Tim had not his sight, Judy herself brought them to the cradle and went to put them on him. She needn't have bothered! The youth seemed quite up to the business. He buckled on the pipes, set the bellows under one arm and the bag under the other, and worked them both as knowingly as if he had been twenty years at the business. He lilted up *Sheela na guira* in the finest style imaginable!

All were in astonishment and the poor Widow Murphey even crossed herself. Tim, who was dark (blind) and did not well know who was playing, was in great delight. When he heard that it was a little *prechan* not five years old and who had never even seen a set of pipes in his life, wished the mother joy of her son. Then he offered to take him off her hands if she would part with him. "He's a piper born!" he swore. "A natural genius. In a little time more, with the help of a little instruction from myself, there will be no match for him in the whole country!"

The poor mother was delighted to hear all this, especially as what Tim said about natural genius. It quieted some misgivings that were rising in her mind, lest what the neighbors said about his not being right might be true. It gratified her, moreover, to think that her dear child (for she really loved the whelp) would not be forced to turn out and beg. He might even earn decent bread for himself! So when Mick came home in the evening from his work, she told him all that had happened and all that Tim Carrol had said. Mick, as was natural, was very glad to hear it, for the helpless condition of his poor son was a great trouble to him. The next day he took his best pig to the fair, and with what it brought set off to Clonmel and ordered a brand new set of pipes, just the right proper size for his boy!

In a fortnight the pipes came home, and the moment the chap in his cradle laid eyes on them he squealed with delight and threw up his legs, bumping himself in the cradle. He went on with a great many comical tricks 'till at last, just to quiet him, they gave him the pipes. He immediately set to and pulled away at *Jig Polthog*, to the admiration of all that heard him.

The fame of his skill on the pipes soon spread far and near, for there was not a piper in the six next counties could come at all near him. He would play the *Old Moderagh rue*, or *The Hare in the Corn*, or *The Fox-Hunters Jig*, or *The Rakes of Cashel*, or the *Piper's Maggot*. Indeed, he could play any of the fine Irish jigs which make people dance whether they will or no! And surprising it was to hear him rattle away *The Fox Hunt*—you'd really think you heard the hounds giving tongue and the terriers yelping behind and the huntsman and the whippers-in cheering or correcting the dogs. It was, in short, the very next thing to seeing the hunt itself.

The best of him was he was no ways stingy at his music. Many a merry dance the boys and girls of the neighborhood used to have in his father's cabin. He would play up music for them that they said used as it were to put quicksilver in their feet. They all declared they never moved so light and so airy to any piper's playing that ever they danced to.

But besides all his fine Irish music, he had one queer tune all of his own—the oddest that ever was heard. The very moment he began to play, everything in the house seemed disposed to dance. The plates and poringers used to jingle on the dresser, the pots and pot-holders used to rattle in the chimney, and people used even to fancy they felt the stools moving under them. But however it might be with the stools, it is certain that no one could keep long sitting on them, for both old and young always fell to capering as hard as ever they could. The girls complained that when he began his tune it always threw them out in their dancing, and that they never could handle their feet rightly, for they felt the floor like ice under them and themselves every moment ready to come sprawling on their backs or their faces. The young bachelors that wished to show off their dancing and their new shoes swore that it confused them so that they never could go rightly through the *heel and toe* or *cover the buckle*, or any of their best steps. They felt themselves always all bedizzied and bewildered, and then old and young would go jostling and knocking together in a frightful manner. And when the unlucky brat had them all in this way, whirligigging about the floor, he'd grin and chuckle and chatter at his roguery.

The Piper Came to Our Town

The older he grew the worse he grew, and by the time he was six years old there was no standing the house for him. He was always making his brothers burn or scald themselves, or break their shins over the pots and stools. One time, in harvest, he was left at home by himself, and when his mother came in she found the cat a horseback on the dog, with her face to the tail and her legs tied around him, and the urchin playing his queer tune to them. The dog went barking and dumping about and Puss was mewing for the dear life, and slapping her tail backwards and forward which, as it would hit against the dog's chaps, he'd snap at and bite and then there was the philliloo!

Another time his mother was coming in from milking the cow, the pail on her head. The minute he saw her he lilted up his infernal tune and the poor woman, letting go the pail, clapped her hands aside and began to dance a jig. The milk tumbled all atop her husband, who was bringing in some turf to boil the supper. In short, there would be no end to telling all his pranks, and all the mischievous tricks he played.

Another time, the farmer for whom Mick worked, a very decent and respectable man, happened to call in and Judy wiped a stool with her apron, inviting him to sit down and rest himself after his walk. He was sitting with his back to the cradle and behind him was a pan of blood, for Judy was making pig's puddings. The lad lay quite still in his nest and watched his opportunity till he got ready a hook at the end of a piece of twine. He contrived to fling so handily that it caught in the bob of the man's nice new hairpiece, and soused it in the pan of blood.

Soon after, some mischances began to happen to the farmer's cattle. A horse took the staggers, a fine veal calf died of the blackleg, and some of his sheep of the red-water. The cows began to grow vicious and to kick down the milk pails, and the roof of one end of the barn fell in. The farmer took it into his head that Mick Flanigan's unlucky child was the cause of the mischief. So one day he called Mick aside and said to him, "Mick, you see things are not going on with me as they ought, and to be plain with you, Mick, I think that child of yours is the cause of it. I am really falling away to nothing with fretting, and I can hardly sleep on my bed at night for thinking of what may happen before the morning. So I'd be glad if you'd look out for work somewhere else; you're as good a man as any in the county, and there's no fear but you'll have your choice of work."

"I'm sorry for your losses," said Mick, "and sorrier still that me or mine should be thought the cause of them. For my own part I am not quite easy in mind about that child, but I had him so I must keep him." Then he promised to look for another place immediately.

Accordingly, next Sunday at chapel Mick gave out that he was about leaving the work at John Riordan's, and immediately a farmer, who lived a couple of miles off and who wanted a ploughman, came up to Mick and offered him a house and garden, and work all the year round. Mick, who knew him to be a good employer, immediately closed with him, so it was agreed that the farmer should send a car to take his little bit of furniture and that he should remove the following Thursday.

When Thursday came, the car came according to promise, and Mick loaded it and put the cradle with the child and his pipes on the top. Judy sat beside it to take care of him, lest he should tumble out and be killed. They drove the cow before them, the dog followed, but the cat was of course left behind. (It is a piece of superstition with the Irish never to take a cat with them when they are removing.) The other three children went along the road picking skeehories and blackberries, for it was a fine day towards the latter end of Harvest.

They had to cross the river, but as it ran through a bottom between two high banks, you did not see it till you were close on it. The young fellow was lying pretty quiet in the bottom of the cradle, till they came to the head of the bridge. When hearing the roaring of the water (for there was a great flood of the river, as it had rained heavily for the last two or three days), he sat up in his cradle and looked about him. The instant he got sight of the water and found they were going to take him across it, oh, how he did bellow and how he did squeal! No rat caught in a snap-trap ever sang out equal to him.

"Whisht! A lanna," said Judy, "there's no fear of you, sure it's only over the stone bridge we're going."

"Bad luck to you, you old rip!" cried he. "What a pretty trick you played on me, to bring me here!" And still he went on yelling, and the further they got on the bridge the louder he yelled, till at last Mick could hold out no longer. He gave him a great skelp of the whip he had in his hand. "Devil choke you, you brat!" said he. "Will you never stop bawling? A body can't hear with ears for you."

The moment he felt the thong of the whip he leaped up in the cradle, clapped the pipes under his arm, gave a most wicked grin at Mick, and jumped clean over the battlements of the bridge down into the water!

"Oh my child, my child!" shouted Judy. "He's gone for ever from me." Mick and the rest of the children ran to the other side of the bridge, and looking over they saw him coming out from under the arch of the bridge, sitting cross-legged on the top of a white-headed wave and playing away on the pipes as merrily as if nothing had happened. The river was running very rapidly, so he was whirled away at a great rate, but he played as fast, ay, and faster, than the river ran. And though they set off as hard as they could along the bank, yet as the river made a sudden turn around the hill, about a hundred yards below the bridge, by the time they got there he was out of sight. No one ever laid eyes on him more, but the general opinion was that he went home with the pipes to his own relations, the Good People, to make music for them.

—Adapted from *Fairy Legends and Traditions of the South of Ireland* by Thomas Crofton Croker, 1882.

—❖—

A customary railer is the devil's bagpipe,
which the world danceth after.
Danish Proverb

The Fairy Teachers

There was a piper on this island, and he had three sons. The two eldest learned the pipes, and they were coming on famously; but the youngest could not learn at all. At last, one day, he was going about in the evening, very sorrowfully, when he saw a *bruth*, a fairy hillock, laid open. He went up to the door, and he struck his knife into it, because he had heard from old people that if he did that, the *sluagh* could not shut the door.

Well, they were very angry, and asked him what he wanted, but he was not a bit afraid. He told them that he could not play the pipes a bit, and asked them to help him. They gave him *Feadan dubh*, a black chanter, but he said, "That's no use to me, for I don't know how to play it."

Then they came about him, and showed him how to move his fingers; that he was to lift this one and lay down that; and when he had been with them a while, he thanked them, and took out his knife, and went away. And the *bruth* closed behind him. Now that man became one of the most famous pipers in __ , and his people were alive till very lately. I'm sure you all know that!

— From *Popular Tales of the West Highlands* by John Francis Campbell, 1893.

— ❖ —

The life of a shepherd is void of all care,
With his bag and his bottle he maketh good fare;
He hath yon green meadow to walk in at will-a,
With a pair of fine bagpipes upon a green hill-a;
Tringdilla, tringdilla, tring down-adown dilla,
With a pair of fine bagpipes upon a green hill-a.
From a 17th-century manuscript, as found in *The Highland Bagpipe* by William Laird Manson, 1901.

Terry O'Roon and His Wonderful Tune

Och! there ne'er was a piper lie Terry O'Roon,
Sure he bother'd them all with his wonderful tune;
And the like of that same, when it came in his head,
It never was equall'd by living or dead.
And this is the reason—a long time ago,
As Terry's own family histories show,
A Fairy once brought to his grandfather's cot
The very same pipes that Terry has got;
"And sure," said his father, who took up the trade,
"St. Patrick himself on the same may have played;"
But none of the pipe-playing house of O'Roon,
Like Terry could strike up the wonderful tune.
    Och, bothering, wheedling Terry O'Roon,
    He charm'd every heart with his wonderful tune.

'Tis said when he struck up his pipes by the shore,
That the fishes danced jigs, and the sea ceased to roar,
That the rocs split with laughing, that herring and sprats
Should foot it with shell-fish, and round fish, and flats;
Be that as it may, Terry swears it's true;
But he might have been dreaming, betwixt me and you;
On a taste of the creature—that caused him ti think,
(For pipers have ever been jewels to drink,)
And Terry himself when the whisky was strong,
He ne'er played so well, nor so loud, nor so long,
Till he set them all dancing—sly Terry O'Roon,
And whatever he play'd 'twas a wonderful tune.
    Och, bothering, wheedling Terry O'Roon,
    He charm'd every heart with his wonderful tune.

There was never a wake, nor a fight, nor a fair,
But Terry O'Roon he was sure to be there;
And many's the match that was made, I'll be bound,
When his wonderful pipes drew the lasses around;
But Terry himself was a rogue, and it's true
It was all one to him whether black eyes or blue;
For when his flirtations some beauty would vex,
"Arrah, honey!" he'd say "ain't I true to the sex?"
And so he went on with his wheedling ways,
And his pipe-playing tricks, to the end of his days;
But there ne'er was a piper like Terry O'Roon,
That was gifted like him with a wonderful tune!
   Och, bothering, wheedling Terry O'Roon,
   Sure he won ev'ry heart with his wonderful tune!

—From *Irish Com-All-Ye's* by Manus O'Conor, 1901.

—❖—

Warlocks and witches in a dance;
Nae cotillion brent-new frae France,
But hornpipes, jigs, strathspeys, and reels
Put life and mettle in their heels.
A winnock bunker in the east,
There sat Auld Nick in shape o' beast:
A towzie tyke, black, grim, and large,
To gie them music was his charge;
He screw'd the pipes and gart them skirl,
Till roof and rafters a' did dirl.
From "Tam O'Shanter" by Robert Burns

The Piper Came to Our Town

Diarmid Bawn, The Piper

One stormy night Patrick Burke was seated in the chimney corner, smoking his pipe quite contentedly after his hard day's work. His two little boys were roasting potatoes in the ashes while his rosy daughter held a splinter (dipped in tallow, and used as a candle) to her mother, who was sitted on a siesteen (straw-seated chair) and mending a rent in Patrick's coat; and Judy, the maid, was singing merrily to the sound of her wheel, that kept up a beautiful humming noise just like the sweet drone of a bagpipe. Indeed, they all seemed quite contented and happy; the storm howled without and they were warm and snug within by the side of a blazing turf fire.

"I was just thinking," said Patrick, taking the dudeen from his mouth and giving it a rap on his thumb nail to shake out the ashes, "I was just thinking how thankful we ought to be to have a snug bit of a cabin over our heads this pelting night, for in all my born days I have never heard the like of this storm!"

"And that's no lie for you, Pat," said his wife Molly. "But whisht!" She dropped her work upon her knees and looked fearfully toward the door. "What a noise is that I heard?"

"The Vargin herself defend us all!" wailed Judy, at the same time rapidly making a pious sign on her forehead. "'Tis not the banshee herself, come to wail our doom!"

"Hold your tongue, you fool!" snapped Patrick.

"It's only the old gate swinging in the wind." Yet he had scarcely spoken when the door was assailed by a violent knocking. Molly began to mumble her prayers and Judy proceeded to mutter over the muster-roll of saints; the youngsters scampered off to hide themselves behind the settle-bed. The storm howled louder and more fiercely than ever, and the rapping on the door was renewed with redoubled violence.

"Whisht! Whisht!" said Patrick, not getting up. "What a noise ye're all making about nothing at all. Judy aroon, can't you go and see who's at the door?" Not withstanding his assumed bravery, Pat Burke preferred that the maid should open the door.

"Why, then, is it me you're speaking to?" said Judy in a tone of astonishment. "And it is cracked mad you are, Mister Burke! Or is it, maybe, that you want me to be run'd away with, and made a horse of like my grandfather was? The sorrow a step will I stir to open the door, if you were as great a man again as you are, Pat Burke."

"Bother you, then! And hold your tongue; I'll go myself." So saying, up got Patrick and made the best of his way to the door. "Who's there?" said he, and his voice trembled mightily all the while. "In the name of Saint Patrick, who's there?"

"'Tis I, Pat," answered a voice which he immediately knew to be the young squire's. He felt a wave of relief, and in a moment had the door opened. In walked a young man with a gun in his hand and a brace of dogs at his heels.

"Your honour's honour is quite welcome, entirely," said Patrick, who was a civil sort of a fellow, especially to those he thought his betters. "Your honour's honour is quite welcome, and if ye'll be so condescending as to demean yourself by taking off your wet jacket, Molly can give ye a bran new blanket. Ye can sit forenent the fire while the clothes are drying."

"Thank you Pat," said the squire as he wrapped himself in the proffered blanket, then sneezed. "But what made you keep me so long at the door?"

"Why, then, your honour," Patrick glanced at his maid, "'Twas Judy, there, being so much afraid of the Good People. And a good right she had, after what happened to her grandfather, the Lord rest his soul!"

"And what was that, Pat?" said the squire.

"Why, then, your honour must know that Judy had a grandfather! He was ould Diarmid Bawn, the Piper! As personable a looking man as any in the five parishes, he was. And he could play the pipes so sweetly, and make them spake to such perfection, that it did one's heart good to hear him. We never had anyone, for that matter, in this side of the country like him, before or since. Except James Gandsey," he added quickly, lest he offend the young squire. "That is our own piper to Lord Headly—his honour's lordship is the real good gentleman. 'Tis Mr. Gandsey's music that is the pride of Killarney Lakes."

"Yes, yes," said the squire, waving his hand. "What of Diarmid?"

"Well, as I was saying, Diarmid was Judy's grandfather, and he rented a small mountainy farm. He was walking about the fields one moonlit night, quite melancholy—like in himself for want of the tobaccy. (The river was flooded and he could not get across to buy any, and Diarmid would rather go to bed without his supper than a whiff of the dudeen.) Well, your honour, just as he came to the old fort in the far field, what should he see—*the Lord preserve us!*—but a large army of the Good People, 'coutered for all the world just like the dragoons. 'Are ye all ready' said a little fellow in the lead, dressed out like a general. 'No,' said a little curmudgeon of a chap all dressed in red, from the crown of his cocked hat to the sole of his boot. 'No general,' said he. 'If you don't get the Fir Darrig a horse he must stay behind, and ye'll lose the battle.'

"'There's Diarmid Bawn' said the general, pointing to Judy's grandfather, your honour, 'Make a horse of him.'

"So with that master Fir Darrig comes up to Diarmid who, you may be sure, was in a mighty great fright. But he determined to put a bold face on the matter, seeing there was no help for him. He began to cross himself, and to say some blessed words that nothing bad could stand before.

"'Is that what you'd be after, you spapeen?' said the little red imp, at the same time grinning a horrible grin; 'I'm not the man to care a straw for either you or your crossings.' So without more a-do, he gives poor Diarmid a rap with the flat side of his sword, and in a moment he was changed into a horse, with little Fir Darrig stuck fast on his back.

"Away they flew over the wide ocean like so many wild geese, screaming and chattering all the time, until they came to Jamaica. There they had a murdering fight with the Good People of that country. Well, it was all very well with them, and they stuck to it manfully and fought it out fairly, till one of the Jamaica men made a cut with his sword under Diarmid's left eye and then, sir, you see, poor Diarmid lost his temper entirely. He dashed to the very middle of them, with Fir Darrig mounted upon his back, and he threw out his heels and whisked his tail about, and wheeled and turned round and round at such a rate that he soon made a fair clearance of them—horse, foot and dragoons! At last Diarmid's faction got the better, all through his means, and they had such a feasting and rejoicing and gave Diarmid, who was the finest horse amongst them, the best of everything.

"'Let every man take a hand of tobaccy for Diarmid Bawn,' said the general, and so they did. Then away they flew to the old fort again, for 'twas getting near morning, and there they vanished like the mist from the mountain.

"When Diarmid looked about the sun was rising, and he thought it was all a dream till he saw a big rick of tobaccy in the old fort, and felt the blood running from his left eye. For sure enough he was wounded in the battle and would have been kilt entirely if it wasn't for a gospel composed by Father Murphey that hung about his neck ever since he had the scarlet fever. For certain it was enough to have given him another scarlet fever to have had the little red man all night on his back, whip and spur for the bare life. However, there was the tobaccy heaped up in a great pile by his side, and he heard a voice, although he could see no one, telling him ''Tis all your own, for your good behavior in the battle. Whenever Fir Darrig has want of a horse again, he'll know where to find a clever beast, as he never rode a better one than you, Diarmid Bawn.' That's what the voice said, sir."

"Thank you, Pat," said the squire. "It certainly is a wonderful story, and I am not surprised at Judy's alarm. But now, seeing as the storm is over and the moon is shining brightly, I'll make the best of my way home." So saying, he disrobed himself of the blanket, put on his coat and, whistling for his dogs, set off across the mountain. Patrick stood in the door, bawling after him, "May God and the blessed Virgin preserve your honour, and keep ye from the Good People, for 'twas a moonlight night like this that Diarmid Bawn was made a horse for the Fir Darrig to ride."

—Adapted from *Fairy Legends and Traditions of the South of Ireland* by Thomas Crofton Croker, 1882.

—❖—

I heard on Christmas Eve the bonny bagpipes play;
The thin silver skirling, it sounded far away;
The yellow mellow light shone through my neighbor's panes,
And on the starry night came the shrill dear strains.
Despite the welter of the wide cold sea,
They brought bonny Scotland across the world to me;
And my heart knew the heather that my sense had never smelt,
And my spirit drank the hill wind my brows had never felt.
From the old kind books came the old friends trooping,
And the old songs called, like the curlew swooping;
And like a sudden sup that was hot and strong and sweet,
The love of bonny Scotland, it ran from head to feet.
O blessings on the heather hills, in white mist or sun!
O blessings on the kind books that make the clans as one!
And blessings on the bagpipes whose magic spanned the sea,
And brought bonny Scotland across the world to me!
"The Christmas Bagpipes" by Helen Gray Cone,
from *The Coat Without a Seam*

Hell's Piper

O have ye heard of Angus Blair,
Who lived long since in black Auchmair?
And have ye heard old pipers tell
His story—how he piped in Hell?
When Angus piped the old grew young,
Crutches across the floor were flung;
Nay, more, 'twas said his witching breath
Had robbed the grave, and cheated death.

Above all else, a march of war
Was what men praised and feared him for;
When that he played, like fire it ran
In blood and brain of every man;
Then stiffened hair began to rise,
Bent brows scowled over staring eyes;
Then, at his will, men spilt their blood
Like water of a winter flood,
Swearing, with Angus, ill or well,
They'd charge light-hearted into Hell.

Long years, through many a feast and fray,
Did piper Angus pipe his way;
Till, swept upon the swirling tide
Of a night-charge, he sank and died.

That night the Piper rose to tread
The ways that lie before the dead.
He saw God's battlements afar
Blazing behind the utmost star,
And turning in the chill night air,
Thought he might find a shelter there.

But as he turned to leave the earth,
With all its music, maids and mirth,
The battered pipes beneath his feet
Screamed out a wailing, last retreat;
Then Piper Angus paused, and thought
Of the wild work those pipes had wrought;
"But there," quoth he, "in peace and rest,
Up there, the holy ones, the blest,
Praise aye the Lord, and aye they sing,
While golden harps and cymbals ring.
To my wild march or mad strathspey
The heavenly host would say me nay,
And none would hear my chanter more
Unless the Lord went out to war.
But often have I heard men tell
How they would follow pipes to Hell.
That way I'll try: in Hell maybe
Some corner's kept for them and me."

So said, so done—for well content,
Down the dark way to Hell he went.
The Chanter felt his finger-tips,
The Blowpipe thrilled between his lips,
The Drones across his shoulder flung,
Moaned till the Earth's foundations rung,
The streamers flaunted on the blast
As, striding smoke and shadow past,
With bonnet cocked, and careless air,
Piping his march, went Piper Blair.

Down where the shackled earthquakes dwell
Are piled the reeking halls of Hell.
Their walls are steel, their gates are brass;
Round them four flaming rivers pass;
And sleepless sentinels are set
On every point and parapet,

To hedge the souls whose far-off cries
Up to the world may never rise.

That night, so still the whole place seemed,
You'd think all Hell had peace, and dreamed,
For the dark Master, brooding aye
Over lost hope and ancient fray,
Had, from his vantage, pale and grim,
Perchance to please a passing whim,
Hissed down a word which quelled an cowed
And silenced all that shuddering crowd.
So now aloft upon his throne,
He sat indifferent, alone,
While poor damned souls, who dared not cry,
In writhing droves went whirling by.
These, dumb, before he noted aught,
Some strange and wandering sound now caught.

And first a little note they heard
Far off—and like a lonely bird;
And then it grew, and grew, and grew,
As near and nearer still it drew,
Until Hell's Lord in slow surprise
Turned on the gates his weary eyes.

Then they that bent beneath a load
Stood up, nor felt the fiery goad.
Then they that trod on forks of flame
Tramped to the wild notes as they came.
Then look, old foes of long ago
Feel old revenge revive and glow.
Then, heedless of the flaming whip,
They roll in one another's grip
With shout and shriek and throttled jeer,
And over all the pipes rang clear.

The Piper Came to Our Town

But from the march those pipes turned soon,
And sank, to sing another tune;
A low lament, whose sobbing wail
Filled aching hearts and made them fail.
And they that fought a breath ago
Now wept at one another's woe.

A second change—a lilting air
Made Hell look bright, made Hell look fair,
And wretches gasping new from death
Followed the tune beneath their breath—
Then piping yet, erect, alone,
The Piper stood before the throne.

Up rose the Master in his place,
Eyeing the Piper's careless face,
"No room, no room in Hell can be
For Piper Angus Blair," cried he;
"Would to such sounds my host had trod
Ere I was hurled down here by God;
Mine hadst thou been before I fell,
I'd rule in Heav'n now—not in Hell.
Then every night and every day
On Heav'n's high ramparts shouldst thou play,
But here—here's neither war nor mirth,
Nor more in Heav'n; so back to Earth."

Thus now, as over glen and brae
The wild wind wanders on its way,
Dead Piper Angus Blair goes too,
And pipes and pipes the whole world through.
Unseen, unknown he goes. Today
He'll pipe perchance for bairns at play
To set them dancing: maybe steal
To-night to watch a roaring reel.
There, when the panting pipers tire,

He joins, and sets all hearts afire;
And ere the dawn his pipes have pealed
Fiercely across some stricken field.
But when each year is at its close
Right down the road to Hell he goes.
There the gaunt porters all a-grin
Fling back the gates to let him in,
Then damned and devil, one and all,
Make mirth and hold high carnival,
The while the Master sits apart
Plotting rebellion in his heart,
Till, when above the dawn is grey,
The Piper turns and tramps away.

—by Riccardo Stephens, from *Lyra Celtica:*
An Anthology of Representative Celtic Poetry,
edited by Elizabeth Sharp, 1876.

—❖—

These are bagpipes. I understand the inventor
of the bagpipes was inspired when he saw a man
carrying an indignant, asthmatic pig under his arm.
Unfortunately, the man-made sound never equalled
the purity of the sound achieved by the pig.
Alfred Hitchcock

The Piper Came to Our Town

The Ratcatcher

There are many hypotheses as to the origin of the legend of the Pied Piper of Hamelin, who led the town's children away to the tune of his bagpipes. Some say the children really left the city as part of a pilgrimage or military campaign; others believe that the children died of some natural cause, and the piper was a symbolic figure of death. Whatever the truth of the matter, there have been many versions of the story all across Europe. This one is from The Red Fairy Book *by Andrew Lang.*

A VERY long time ago the town of Hamel in Germany was invaded by bands of rats, the like of which had never been seen before nor will ever be again.

They were great black creatures that ran boldly in broad daylight through the streets, and swarmed so, all over the houses, that people at last could not put their hand or foot down anywhere without touching one. When dressing in the morning they found them in their breeches and petticoats, in their pockets and in their boots; and when they wanted a morsel to eat, the voracious horde had swept away everything from cellar to garret. The night was even worse. As soon as the lights were out, these untiring nibblers set to work. And everywhere, in the ceilings, in the floors, in the cupboards, at the doors, there was a chase and a rummage, and so furious a noise of gimlets, pincers, and saws, that a deaf man could not have rested for one hour together.

Neither cats nor dogs, nor poison nor traps, nor prayers nor candles burnt to all the saints—nothing would do anything. The more they killed the more came. And the inhabitants of Hamel began to go to the dogs (not that THEY were of much use), when one Friday there arrived in the town a man with a queer face, who played the bagpipes and sang this refrain:

'*Qui vivra verra:*
Le voila,
Le preneur des rats.'

He was a great gawky fellow, dry and bronzed, with a crooked nose, a long rat-tail moustache, two great yellow piercing and mocking eyes, under a large felt hat set off by a scarlet cock's feather. He was dressed in a green jacket with a leather belt and red breeches, and on his feet were sandals fastened by thongs passed round his legs in the gipsy fashion.

That is how he may be seen to this day, painted on a window of the cathedral of Hamel.

He stopped on the great market-place before the town hall, turned his back on the church and went on with his music, singing:

'Who lives shall see:
This is he,
The ratcatcher.'

The town council had just assembled to consider once more this plague of Egypt, from which no one could save the town.

The stranger sent word to the counsellors that, if they would make it worth his while, he would rid them of all their rats before night, down to the very last.

'Then he is a sorcerer!' cried the citizens with one voice; 'we must beware of him.'

The Town Counsellor, who was considered clever, reassured them. He said: 'Sorcerer or no, if this bagpiper speaks the truth, it was he who sent us this horrible vermin that he wants to rid us of to-day for money. Well, we must learn to catch the devil in his own snares. You leave it to me.'

'Leave it to the Town Counsellor,' said the citizens one to another.

And the stranger was brought before them.

'Before night,' said he, 'I shall have despatched all the rats in Hamel if you will but pay me a gros a head.'

'A gros a head!' cried the citizens, 'but that will come to millions of florins!'

The Town Counsellor simply shrugged his shoulders and said

The Piper Came to Our Town

to the stranger:

'A bargain! To work; the rats will be paid one gros a head as you ask.'

The bagpiper announced that he would operate that very evening when the moon rose. He added that the inhabitants should at that hour leave the streets free, and content themselves with looking out of their windows at what was passing, and that it would be a pleasant spectacle. When the people of Hamel heard of the bargain, they too exclaimed: 'A gros a head! but this will cost us a deal of money!'

'Leave it to the Town Counsellor,' said the town council with a malicious air. And the good people of Hamel repeated with their counsellors, 'Leave it to the Town Counsellor.'

Towards nine at night the bagpiper re-appeared on the market place. He turned, as at first, his back to the church, and the moment the moon rose on the horizon, 'Trarira, trari!' the bagpipes resounded.

It was first a slow, caressing sound, then more and more lively and urgent, and so sonorous and piercing that it penetrated as far as the farthest alleys and retreats of the town.

Soon from the bottom of the cellars, the top of the garrets, from under all the furniture, from all the nooks and corners of the houses, out come the rats, search for the door, fling themselves into the street, and trip, trip, trip, begin to run in file towards the front of the town hall, so squeezed together that they covered the pavement like the waves of flooded torrent.

When the square was quite full the bagpiper faced about, and, still playing briskly, turned towards the river that runs at the foot of the walls of Hamel.

Arrived there he turned round; the rats were following.

'Hop! hop!' he cried, pointing with his finger to the middle of the stream, where the water whirled and was drawn down as if through a funnel. And hop! hop! without hesitating, the rats took the leap, swam straight to the funnel, plunged in head foremost and disappeared.

The plunging continued thus without ceasing till midnight.

At last, dragging himself with difficulty, came a big rat, white with age, and stopped on the bank.

It was the king of the band.

'Are they all there, friend Blanchet?' asked the bagpiper.

'They are all there,' replied friend Blanchet.

'And how many were they?'

'Nine hundred and ninety thousand, nine hundred and ninety-nine.'

'Well reckoned?'

'Well reckoned.'

'Then go and join them, old sire, and au revoir.'

Then the old white rat sprang in his turn into the river, swam to the whirlpool and disappeared.

When the bagpiper had thus concluded his business he went to bed at his inn. And for the first time during three months the people of Hamel slept quietly through the night.

The next morning, at nine o'clock, the bagpiper repaired to the town hall, where the town council awaited him.

'All your rats took a jump into the river yesterday,' said he to the counsellors, 'and I guarantee that not one of them comes back. They were nine hundred and ninety thousand, nine hundred and ninety-nine, at one gros a head. Reckon!'

'Let us reckon the heads first. One gros a head is one head the gros. Where are the heads?'

The ratcatcher did not expect this treacherous stroke. He paled with anger and his eyes flashed fire.

'The heads!' cried he, 'if you care about them, go and find them in the river.'

'So,' replied the Town Counsellor, 'you refuse to hold to the terms of your agreement? We ourselves could refuse you all payment. But you have been of use to us, and we will not let you go without a recompense,' and he offered him fifty crowns.

'Keep your recompense for yourself,' replied the ratcatcher proudly. 'If you do not pay me I will be paid by your heirs.'

Thereupon he pulled his hat down over his eyes, went hastily out of the hall, and left the town without speaking to a soul.

The Piper Came to Our Town

When the Hamel people heard how the affair had ended they rubbed their hands, and with no more scruple than their Town Counsellor, they laughed over the ratcatcher, who, they said, was caught in his own trap. But what made them laugh above all was his threat of getting himself paid by their heirs. Ha! they wished that they only had such creditors for the rest of their lives.

Next day, which was a Sunday, they all went gaily to church, thinking that after Mass they would at last be able to eat some good thing that the rats had not tasted before them.

They never suspected the terrible surprise that awaited them on their return home. No children anywhere, they had all disappeared!

'Our children! Where are our poor children?' was the cry that was soon heard in all the streets.

Then through the east door of the town came three little boys, who cried and wept, and this is what they told:

While the parents were at church a wonderful music had resounded. Soon all the little boys and all the little girls that had been left at home had gone out, attracted by the magic sounds, and had rushed to the great market-place. There they found the ratcatcher playing his bagpipes at the same spot as the evening before. Then the stranger had begun to walk quickly, and they had followed, running, singing and dancing to the sound of the music, as far as the foot of the mountain which one sees on entering Hamel. At their approach the mountain had opened a little, and the bagpiper had gone in with them, after which it had closed again. Only the three little ones who told the adventure had remained outside, as if by a miracle. One was bandy-legged and could not run fast enough; the other, who had left the house in haste, one foot shod the other bare, had hurt himself against a big stone and could not walk without difficulty; the third had arrived in time, but in harrying to go in with the others had struck so violently against the wall of the mountain that he fell backwards at the moment it closed upon his comrades.

At this story the parents redoubled their lamentations. They ran with pikes and mattocks to the mountain, and searched till evening to find the opening by which their children had disappeared, without being able to find it. At last, the night falling, they returned desolate to Hamel.

But the most unhappy of all was the Town Counsellor, for he lost three little boys and two pretty little girls, and to crown all, the people of Hamel overwhelmed him with reproaches, forgetting that the evening before they had all agreed with him.

What had become of all these unfortunate children?

The parents always hoped they were not dead, and that the ratcatcher, who certainly must have come out of the mountain, would have taken them with him to his country. That is why for several years they sent in search of them to different countries, but no one ever came on the trace of the poor little ones.

It was not till much later that anything was to be heard of them.

About one hundred and fifty years after the event, when there was no longer one left of the fathers, mothers, brothers or sisters of that day, there arrived one evening in Hamel some merchants of Bremen returning from the East, who asked to speak with the citizens. They told that they, in crossing Hungary, had sojourned in a mountainous country called Transylvania, where the inhabitants only spoke German, while all around them nothing was spoken but Hungarian. These people also declared that they came from Germany, but they did not know how they chanced to be in this strange country. 'Now,' said the merchants of Bremen, 'these Germans cannot be other than the descendants of the lost children of Hamel.'

The people of Hamel did not doubt it; and since that day they regard it as certain that the Transylvanians of Hungary are their country folk, whose ancestors, as children, were brought there by the ratcatcher. There are more difficult things to believe than that.

—From *The Red Fairy Book* by Andrew Lang, 1895.

Tom Tit Tot

Tom, he was a piper's son,
He learnt to play when he was young,
And all the tune that he could play,
Was, "Over the Hills and Far Away"!
> *Over the hills and a great way off,*
> *The wind shall blow my top-knot off!*

Now Tom with his pipes made such a noise,
That he pleased both the girls and boys,
They all danced while he did play,
"Over the Hills and Far Away."
> *Over the hills and a great way off,*
> *The wind shall blow my top-knot off!*

Tom with his pipes did play with such skill
That those who heard him could never keep still;
As soon as he played they began to dance
Even pigs on their hind legs would prance.
> *Over the hills and a great way off,*
> *The wind shall blow my top-knot off!*

As Dolly was milking her cow one day,
Tom took his pipe and began to play,
So Doll and the cow danced "The Cheshire Round,"
Till the pail was broke and the milk ran aground.
> *Over the hills and a great way off,*
> *The wind shall blow my top-knot off!*

He met old Dame Trot with a basket of eggs,
He used his pipe and she used her legs;
She danced about till the eggs were all broke,
She began for to fret, but he laughed at the joke.
> *Over the hills and a great way off,*
> *The wind shall blow my top-knot off!*

The Piper Came to Our Town

Tom saw a cross fellow was beating an ass,
Heavy laden with pots, pans, dishes and glass;
He took out his pipe and he played them a tune,
And the poor donkey's load was lightened full soon.
Over the hills and a great way off,
The wind shall blow my top-knot off!

—Traditional nursery rhyme. The text is based on the version
found in *Favourite Rhymes for the Nursery*, published by
T. Nelson and Sons, Edinburgh, 1887.

— ❖ —

Tom, Tom, the Piper's Son
Stole a pig and away did run.
The pig was eat and Tom was beat
Till he ran crying down the street.
Traditional

The Last Piper

Dark winds of the mountain,
White winds of the sea,
Are skirling the pibroch
Of Seumas an Righ.

The crying of gannets,
The shrieking of terns,
Are keening his dying
High over the burns.

Grey silence of waters
And wasting of lands
And the wailing of music
Down to the sands.

The wailing of music,
And trailing of wind,
The waters before him,
The mountains behind,—

Alone at the gathering,
Silent he stands,
And the wail of his piping
Cries over the lands,

To the moan of the waters,
The drone of the foam,
Where his soul, a white gannet,
Wings silently home.

—by Edward J. O'Brien, *The Second Book of Modern Verse*,
edited by Jessie B. Rittenhouse, 1922.

The Fisher

A fisher once took his bagpipes to the bank of a river, and played upon them with the hope of making the fish rise; but never a one put his nose out of the water. So he cast his net into the river and soon drew it forth filled with fish. Then he took his bagpipes again, and, as he played, the fish leapt up in the net. "Ah, you dance now when I play," said he.

"Yes," said an old Fish:

WHEN YOU ARE IN A MAN'S POWER
YOU MUST DO AS HE BIDS YOU.

—From *Æsop's Fables, The Harvard Classics,* 1909–14.

—❖—

Melancholy...as the drone
of Lincolnshire bagpipes.
William Shakespeare

The Changeling and His Bagpipes

A certain youth whom we shall here distinguish by the name of Rickard the Rake, amply earned his title by the time he lost in fair-tents, in dance-houses, in following hunts, and other unprofitable occupations, leaving his brothers and his aged father to attend to the concerns of the farm, or neglect them as they pleased.

It is indispensable to the solemnities of a night dance in the country, to take the barn door off its hinges, and lay it on the floor to test the skill of the best dancers in the room in a single performance. In this was Rickard eminent, and many an evening did he hold the eyes of the assembly intent on his flourishes, lofty springs and kicks, and the other fashionable variations taught by the departed race of dancing-masters.

One evening while earning the applause of the admiring crowd, he uttered a cry of pain, and fell on his side on the hard door. A wonderful scene of confusion ensued—the groans of the dancer, the pitying exclamations of the crowd, and their endeavours to stifle the sufferer in their eagerness to comfort him. We must suppose him carried home and confined to his bed for weeks, the complaint being a stiffness in one of his hip joints, occasioned by a fairy-dart. Fairy-doctors, male and female, tried their herbs and charms on him in vain; and more than one on leaving the house said to one of his family, "God send it's not one of the sheeoges yous are nursing, instead of poor wild Rickard!"

And indeed there seemed to be some reason in the observation. The jovial, reckless, good-humoured buck was now a meagre, disagreeable, exacting creature, with pinched features, and harsh voice, and craving appetite; and for several weeks he continued to plague and distress his unfortunate family. By the advice of a fairyman a pair of bagpipes was accidentally left near his bed, and ears were soon on the stretch to catch the dulcet notes of the instrument from the room. It was well known that he was not at all skilled in the musical art; so if a well-played tune were heard from under his fingers, the course to be adopted by this family was clear.

But the invalid was as crafty as they were cunning; groans of pain and complaints of neglect formed the only body of sound that issued from the sick chamber. At last, during a hot harvest afternoon when every one should be in the field, and a dead silence reigned through the house, and yard, and out-offices, some one that was watching from an unsuspected press saw an anxious, foxy face peep out from the gently opened door of the room, and draw itself back after a careful survey of the great parlour into which it opened, and which had the large kitchen on the other side. Soon after, the introductory squeal of the instrument was heard, but of a sweeter quality than the same pipes ever uttered before or after that day. Then followed a strain of such wild and sweet melody as held in silent rapture about a dozen of the people of the house and some neighbours who had been apprised of the experiment, and who, till the first enchanting sound breathed through the house, had kept themselves quiet in the room above the kitchen, consequently the farthest from the changeling's station.

While they stood or sat entranced as air succeeded to air, and the last still the sweetest, they began to distinguish whispers, and the nearly inaudible rustle of soft and gauzy dresses seemingly brushing against each other, and such subdued sounds as a cat's feet might cause, swiftly pacing along a floor. They were unable to stir, or even move their lips, so powerful was the charm of the fairy's music on their wills and their senses, till at last the fairy-man spoke—the only person who had the will or the capacity to hold conference with him being the fairy-woman from the next townland.

He.—Come, come! this must be put a stop to.

The words were not all uttered when a low whistling noise was heard from the next room, and the moment after there was profound stillness.

The Piper Came to Our Town

She.—Yes, indeed; and what would you advise us to do first with the anointed sheeoge?

He.—We'll begin easy. We'll take him neck and crop and hold his head under the water in the turnhole till we'll dhrive the divel out of him.

She.—That 'ud be a great deal too easy a punishment for the thief. We'll hate the shovel red-hot, put it under his currabingo, and land him out in the dung-lough.

He.—Ah, now; can't you thry easier punishments on him? I'll put the tongs in the fire till the claws are as hot as the divel, and won't I hould his nasty crass nose between them till he'll know the difference between a fiery faces and a latchycock.[1]

She.—No, no! Say nothing, and I'll go and bring my liquor, drawn from the leaves of the lussmore;[2] and if he was a sheeoge forty times, it will put the inside of him into such a state that he'd give the world he could die. Some parts of him will be as if he had red-hot saws rasping him asunder, and others as if needles of ice were crossing and crossing each other in his bowels; and when he's dead, we'll give him no better grave nor the bog-hole, or the outside of the churchyard.

He.—Very well; let's begin. I'll bring my red-hot tongs from the kitchen fire, and you your little bottle of lussmore water. Don't any of yez go in, neighbours, till we have them ingradients ready.

There was a pause in the outer room while the fairy man passed into the kitchen and back. Then there was a rush at the door, and a bursting into the room; but there was no sign of the changeling on the bed, nor under the bed, nor in any part of the room. At last one of the women shouted out in terror, for the face of the fiend was seen at the window, looking in, with such scorn and hate on the fearful features as struck terror into the boldest. However, the fairy man dashed at him with his burning tongs in hand; but just as it was on the point of gripping his nose, a some-

---

1. Attempts at two law terms. The author has been acquainted with peasants to whom law terms and processes were as familiar as ever they were to poor Peter Peebles.

2. Great Herb. The Purpureus Digitalis, Fairy-finger, or Foxglove.

thing between a laugh and a scream, that made the blood in their veins run cold, came from him. Face and all vanished, and that was the last that was seen of him. Next morning, Rickard, now a reformed rake, was found in his own bed. Great was the joy at his recovery, and great it continued, for he laid aside his tobacco-pipe and pint and quart measures. He forsook the tent and the shee-been house, and took kindly to his reaping-hook, his spade, his plough, and his prayer-book, and blessed the night he was fairy-struck on the dance floor.

—From *Legendary Fiction of the Irish Celts* by Patrick Kennedy, 1891.

—❖—

Amaz'd and curious,
The mirth and fun grew fast and furious:
The piper loud and louder blew,
The dancers quick and quicker flew;
They reel'd, they set, they cross'd, they cleekit,
Till ilka carline swat and reekit.
From "Tam o' Shanter" by Robert Burns

Barrett the Piper

Barrett the Piper, you see, lost his skill, and was advised to go to the Black North to recover it (Barrett was a Munster man). Well, he took his little boy with him and they walked and they walked till the dark came, and they went into a cabin by the roadside to look for lodging. "God save all here!" says they.

"Save you kindly!" says the man of the house, but he left out the Holy Name. "How are you, Jack Barrett?"

"Musha, pure and hearty, sir; many thanks for the axing, but how did you know me?"

"Och, I knew you before you were weaned. Sit down and make yourself at home; here you stay till morning."

Well, faith, they got a good supper of pytatees and milk, and a good bed of straw was made for them by the wall up near the fire, and they lay down quite comfortable to get a good sleep. But some bad thoughts came over Jack Barrett in the dead of the night, and he got up and went out of the bed, and it's in the fields he found himself, and a couple of mad dogs running after him. There was a big tree near him with ever so many crows' nests in the top, and he run and climbed up in it from the dogs, and if he missed the dogs he found the crows, and didn't they fall on him to tear his eyes out! He bawled, and he roared, and the man of the house came into the kitchen, and stirred the fire, and there was Jack Barrett on the hen-roost, and the cocks and hens cackling about him.

"Musha, the sorra's on you for a Jack Barrett! How did you get up there among the fowl?"

"The goodness knows; it's not their company I want. Will you help me down, honest man?"

Well, he got into bed again, and if he did he was not long there when a bad thought come into his head, and up he got. He was going into the next room, when where did he find himself but by the bank of a big river, and the same two dogs tearing along like vengeance to make gibbets of him. There was a tree there, and its boughs were out over the river. Up climbs Jack, and up after him with the dogs; and to get out of their clutches he scrambled out on a long bough. The dogs were soon feeling after him, and he going out farther and farther, till he was afraid it would break. At last he felt it cracking, and he gave a roar out of him that you'd hear a mile off, and the man of the house came into the kitchen, and stirred the fire, and there was Jack sthraddle-leg on the pot-rack.

"Musha, Jack, but you're the devil's quare youth at your time o' life to be makin' a horse of my pot-rack. Come down, you onshuch, and go to bed."

Well, the third time, where did the divel guide him but to a bed in the next room, and when he flopped into it, he let such a yowl out of him that you'd think it was heaven and earth was coming together.

"What's in the win' now, Jack?" says the man o' the house.

"Oh, it's in the pains of labour I am," says the unfortunate piper.

"Will we send for the midwife for you?" says the other.

"Oh, the curse o' Cromwell on yourself an' the midwife!" says the poor man; "it wasn't God had a hand in us the hour we darkened your door. Oh, tattheration to you, you ould thief! Won't you give us some aise?"

"Father honey," says the boy, "it's pishrogues is an you. A drop of holy water will do you more good nor the master o' the house, God bless him!"

"I'll tear you limb from limb," says the ould villain when he heard the Holy Name, "if you say that again."

"Well, anyhow," says the boy, "make the sign of the cross on yourself, father, and say the Lord's Prayer." The poor ould piper did so, and at the blessed words and the sign, his pains left him. There was no sight of the man of the house on the spot then; maybe he was in the lower room. When the piper and his son woke next morning, they were lying in the dry moat of an ould rath that lay by the high road.

—From *Legendary Fiction of the Irish Celts* by Patrick Kennedy, 1891. Originally titled "The Misfortunes of Barrett the Piper."

The Piper Came to Our Town

Mr. Vinegar

MR. and Mrs. Vinegar lived in a vinegar bottle. Now, one day, when Mr. Vinegar was from home, Mrs. Vinegar, who was a very good housewife, was busily sweeping her house, when an unlucky thump of the broom brought the whole house cutter-clatter, cutter-clatter, about her ears. In an agony of grief she rushed forth to meet her husband. On seeing him she exclaimed, 'O Mr. Vinegar, Mr. Vinegar, we are ruined, we are ruined. I have knocked the house down, and it is all to pieces!' Mr. Vinegar then said: 'My dear, let us see what can be done. Here is the door; I will take it on my back, and we will go forth to seek our fortune.' They walked all that day, and at nightfall entered a thick forest. They were both very, very tired, and Mr. Vinegar said: 'My love, I will climb up into a tree, drag up the door, and you shall follow.' He accordingly did so, and they both stretched their weary limbs on the door, and fell asleep.

In the middle of the night, Mr. Vinegar was disturbed by the sound of voices underneath and to his horror and dismay found that it was a band of thieves met to divide their booty. 'Here, Jack,' said one, 'there's five pounds for you; here, Bill, here's ten pounds for you; here, Bob, there's three pounds for you.' Mr. Vinegar could listen no longer; his terror was so great that he trembled and trembled, and shook down the door on their heads. Away scampered the thieves, but Mr. Vinegar dared not quit his retreat till broad daylight. He then scrambled out of the tree, and went to lift up the door. What did he see but a number of golden guineas. 'Come down, Mrs. Vinegar,' he cried; 'come down, I say; our fortune's made, our fortune's made! Come down, I say.'

Mrs. Vinegar got down as fast as she could, and when she saw the money, she jumped for joy. 'Now, my dear,' said she, 'I'll tell you what you shall do. There is a fair at the neighbouring town; you shall take these forty guineas and buy a cow. I can make butter and cheese, which you shall sell at market, and we shall then be able to live very comfortably.'

Mr. Vinegar joyfully agrees, takes the money, and off he goes to the fair. When he arrived, he walked up and down, and at length saw a beautiful red cow. It was an excellent milker, and perfect in every way. 'Oh!' thought Mr. Vinegar, 'if I had but that cow, I should be the happiest man alive.' So he offered the forty guineas for the cow, and the owner said that, as he was a friend, he'd oblige him. So the bargain was made, and he got the cow and he drove it backwards and forwards to show it.

By and by he saw a man playing the bagpipes—*Tweedle-dum, tweedle-dee*. The children followed him about, and he appeared to be pocketing money on all sides. 'Well,' thought Mr. Vinegar, 'if I had but that beautiful instrument I should be the happiest man alive; my fortune would be made.' So he went up to the man. 'Friend,' says he, 'what a beautiful instrument that is, and what a deal of money you must make.' 'Why, yes,' said the man, 'I make a great deal of money, to be sure, and it is a wonderful instrument.' 'Oh!' cried Mr. Vinegar, 'how I should like to possess it!' 'Well,' said the man, 'as you are a friend, I don't much mind parting with it: you shall have it for that red cow.' 'Done!' said the delighted Mr. Vinegar.

So the beautiful red cow was given for the bagpipes. He walked up and down with his purchase; but it was in vain he tried to play a tune, and instead of pocketing pence, the boys followed him hooting, laughing, and pelting.

Poor Mr. Vinegar, his fingers grew very cold, and, just as he was leaving the town, he met a man with a fine thick pair of gloves. 'Oh, my fingers are so very cold,' said Mr. Vinegar to himself. 'Now if I had but those beautiful gloves I should be the happiest man alive.' He went up to the man, and said to him: 'Friend, you seem to have a capital pair of gloves there.' 'Yes, truly,' cried the man; 'and my hands are as warm as possible this cold November day.' 'Well,' said Mr. Vinegar, 'I should like to have them.' 'What will you give?' said the man; 'as you are a friend, I don't much mind letting you have them for those bagpipes.' 'Done!' cried Mr. Vinegar. He put

The Piper Came to Our Town

on the gloves, and felt perfectly happy as he trudged homewards.

At last he grew very tired, when he saw a man coming towards him with a good stout stick in his hand.

'Oh,' said Mr. Vinegar, 'that I had but that stick! I should then be the happiest man alive.' He said to the man: 'Friend, what a rare good stick you have got!' 'Yes,' said the man; 'I have used it for many a long mile, and a good friend it has been; but if you have a fancy for it, as you are a friend, I don't mind giving it to you for that pair of gloves.' Mr Vinegar's hands were so warm, and his legs so tired, that he gladly made the exchange.

As he drew near to the wood where he had left his wife, he heard a parrot on a tree calling out his name: 'Mr. Vinegar, you foolish man, you blockhead, you simpleton; you went to the fair, and laid out all your money in buying a cow. Not content with that, you changed it for bagpipes, on which you could not play, and which were not worth one-tenth of the money. You fool, you— you had no sooner got the bagpipes than you changed them for the gloves, which were not worth one-quarter of the money; and when you had got the gloves, you changed them for a poor miserable stick; and now for your forty guineas, cow, bagpipes, and gloves, you have nothing to show but that poor miserable stick, which you might have cut in any hedge.'

On this the bird laughed and laughed, and Mr. Vinegar, falling into a violent rage, threw the stick at its head. The stick lodged in the tree, and he returned to his wife without money, cow, bagpipes, gloves, or stick, and she instantly gave him such a sound cudgelling that she almost broke every bone in his skin.

—From *English Fairy Tales* by Joseph Jacobs, 1890. Jacobs was a well-known folklorist and historian whose works include *European Folk and Fairy Tales*, *Indian Fairy Tales*, *Celtic Fairy Tales*, and *English Fairy Tales*, from which this story comes.

The Dragon and the Prince

Versions of this story can be found across Russia and Eastern Europe. This Serbian spin on the tale is from Sixty Folk-Tales from Exclusively Slavonic Sources *by Albert Henry Wratislaw.*

There was an emperor who had three sons. One day the eldest son went out hunting, and when he got outside the town, up sprang a hare out of a bush, and he after it, and hither and thither, till the hare fled into a water-mill, and the prince after it. But it was not a hare, but a dragon, and it waited for the prince and devoured him.

When several days had elapsed and the prince did not return home, people began to wonder why it was that he was not to be found. Then the middle son went hunting, and as he issued from the town, a hare sprang out of a bush, and the prince after it, and hither and thither, till the hare fled into the water-mill and the prince after it; but it was not a hare, but a dragon, which waited for and devoured him.

When some days had elapsed and the princes did not return, either of them, the whole court was in sorrow. Then the third son went hunting, to see whether he could not find his brothers. When he issued from the town, again up sprang a hare out of a bush, and the prince after it, and hither and thither, till the hare fled into the water-mill. But the prince did not choose to follow it, but went to find other game, saying to himself: "When I return I shall find you."

After this he went for a long time up and down the hill, but found nothing, and then returned to the water-mill; but when he got there, there was only an old woman in the mill. The prince invoked God in addressing her: "God help you, old woman!" The old woman replied: "God help you, my son!" Then the prince asked her: "Where, old woman, is my hare?" She replied: "My son, that was not a hare, but a dragon. It kills and throttles many people." Hearing this, the prince was somewhat disturbed, and said to the old woman: "What shall we do now? Doubtless my two brothers also have perished here." The old woman answered: "They have indeed; but there's no help for it. Go home, my son, lest you follow them." Then he said to her: "Dear old woman, do you know what? I know that you will be glad to liberate yourself from that pest." The old woman interrupted him: "How should I not? It captured me, too, in this way, but now I have no means of escape."

Then he proceeded: "Listen well to what I am going to say to you. Ask it whither it goes and where its strength is; then kiss all that place where it tells you its strength is, as if from love, till you ascertain it, and afterwards tell me when I come." Then the prince went off to the palace, and the old woman remained in the water-mill.

When the dragon came in, the old woman began to question it: "Where in God's name have you been? Whither do you go so far? You will never tell me whither you go." The dragon replied: "Well, my dear old woman, I do go far." Then the old woman began to coax it: "And why do you go so far? Tell me where your strength is. If I knew where your strength is, I don't know what I should do for love; I would kiss all that place." Thereupon the dragon smiled and said to her: "Yonder is my strength, in that fireplace." Then the old woman began to fondle and kiss the fireplace, and the dragon on seeing it burst into a laugh, and said to her: "Silly old woman, my strength isn't there; my strength is in that tree-fungus in front of the house." Then the old woman began again to fondle and kiss the tree, and the dragon again laughed, and said to her: "Away, old woman! my strength isn't there." Then the old woman inquired: "Where is it?" The dragon began to give an account in detail:

"My strength is a long way off, and you cannot go thither. Far in another empire under the emperor's city is a lake, in that lake is a dragon, and in the dragon a boar, and in the boar a pigeon, and in that is my strength."

The next morning when the dragon went away from the mill, the prince came to the old woman, and the old woman told him all that she had heard from the dragon. Then he left his home, and disguised himself; he put shepherd's boots on his feet, took a shepherd's staff in his hand, and went into the world. As he went on thus from village to village, and from town to town, at last he came into another empire and into the imperial city, in a lake under which the dragon was.

On going into the town, he began to inquire who wanted a shepherd. The citizens told him that the emperor did. Then he went straight to the emperor. After he announced himself, the emperor admitted him into his presence, and asked him: "Do you wish to keep sheep?" He replied: "I do, illustrious crown!" Then the emperor engaged him, and began to inform and instruct him: "There is here a lake, and alongside of the lake very beautiful pasture, and when you call the sheep out, they go thither at once, and spread themselves round the lake; but whatever shepherd goes off there, that shepherd returns back no more. Therefore, my son, I tell you, don't let the sheep have their own way and go where they will, but keep them where you will."

The prince thanked the emperor, got himself ready, and called out the sheep, taking with him, moreover, two hounds that could catch a boar in the open country, and a falcon that could capture any bird, and carrying also a pair of bagpipes.

When he called out the sheep he let them go at once to the lake, and when the sheep arrived at the lake, they immediately spread round it, and the prince placed the falcon on a stump, and the hounds and bagpipes under the stump, then tucked up his hose and sleeves, waded into the lake, and began to shout "Dragon! Dragon! Come out to single combat with me to-day that we may measure ourselves together, unless you're a woman."

The dragon called out in reply, "I will do so now, prince—now!" Erelong, behold the dragon! It is large, it is terrible, it is disgusting! When the dragon came out, it seized him by the waist, and they wrestled a summer day till afternoon. But when the heat of afternoon came on, the dragon said: "Let me go, prince, that I may moisten my parched head in the lake, and toss you to the sky." But the prince replied: "Come, dragon, don't talk nonsense; if I had the emperor's daughter to kiss me on the forehead, I would toss you still higher." Thereupon the dragon suddenly let go of him, and went off into the lake.

On the approach of evening, he washed and got himself up nicely, placed the falcon on his arm, the hounds behind him, and the bagpipes under his arm, then drove the sheep and went into the town playing on the bagpipes. When he arrived at the town, the whole town assembled as to see a wondrous sight because he had come, whereas previously no shepherd had been able to come from the lake.

The next day the prince got ready again, and went with his sheep straight to the lake. But the emperor sent two grooms after him to go stealthily and see what he did, and they placed themselves on a high hill whence they could have a good view. When the shepherd arrived, he put the hounds and bagpipes under the stump and the falcon upon it, then tucked up his hose and sleeves, waded into the lake and shouted: "Dragon, dragon! Come out to single combat with me, that we may measure ourselves once more together, unless you are a woman!" The dragon replied: "I will do so, prince; now, now!" Erelong, behold the dragon! It was large, it was terrible, it was disgusting! And it seized him by the waist and wrestled with him a summer's day till afternoon. But when the afternoon heat came on, the dragon said: "Let me go, prince, that I may moisten my parched head in the lake, and may toss you to the sky." The prince replied: "Come, dragon, don't talk nonsense; if I had the emperor's daughter to kiss me on the forehead, I would toss you still higher." Thereupon the dragon suddenly left hold of him, and went off into the lake.

When night approached the prince drove the sheep as before, and went home playing the bagpipes. When he arrived at the town, the whole town was astir and began to wonder because the shepherd came home every evening, which no one had been able to do before. Those two grooms had already arrived at the palace before the prince, and related to the emperor in order everything that they had heard and seen.

Now when the emperor saw that the shepherd returned home, he immediately summoned his daughter into his presence and told her all, what it was and how it was. "But," said he, "to-morrow you must go with the shepherd to the lake and kiss him on the forehead." When she heard this she burst into tears and began to entreat her father. "You have no one but me, and I am your only daughter, and you don't care about me if I perish." Then the emperor began to persuade and encourage her: "Don't fear, my daughter; you see, we have had so many changes of shepherds, and of all that went out to the lake not one has returned; but he has been contending with the dragon for two whole days and it has done him no hurt. I assure you, in God's name, that he is able to overcome the dragon, only go to-morrow with him to see whether he will free us from this mischief which has destroyed so many people."

When, on the morrow, the day dawned, the day dawned and the sun came forth, up rose the shepherd, up rose the maiden too, to begin to prepare for going to the lake. The shepherd was cheerful, more cheerful than ever, but the emperor's daughter was sad, and shed tears. The shepherd comforted her: "Lady sister, I pray you, do not weep, but do what I tell you. When it is time, run up and kiss me, and fear not."

As he went and drove the sheep, the shepherd was thoroughly cheery, and played a merry tune on his bagpipes; but the damsel did nothing but weep as she went beside him, and he several times left off playing and turned towards her: "Weep not, golden one; fear nought."

When they arrived at the lake, the sheep immediately spread round it, and the prince placed the falcon on the stump, and the hounds and bagpipes under it, then tucked up his hose and sleeves, waded into the water, and shouted: "Dragon! dragon! Come out to single combat with me; let us measure ourselves once more, unless you're a woman!" The dragon replied: "I will, prince; now, now!" Erelong, there was the dragon! It was huge, it was terrible, it was disgusting! When it came out, they seized each other by the middle, and wrestled a summer's day till afternoon. But when the afternoon heat came on, the dragon said: "Let me go, prince, that I may moisten my parched head in the lake, and toss you to the skies." The prince replied "Come, dragon, don't talk nonsense; if I had the emperor's daughter to kiss me on the forehead, I would toss you much higher." When he said this, the emperor's daughter ran up and kissed him on the face, on the eye, and on the forehead. Then he swung the dragon, and tossed it high into the air, and when it fell to the ground it burst into pieces. But as it burst into pieces, out of it sprang a wild boar, and started to run away. But the prince shouted to his shepherd dogs: "Hold it! Don't let it go!" and the dogs sprang up and after it, caught it, and soon tore it to pieces. But out of the boar flew a pigeon, and the prince loosed the falcon, and the falcon caught the pigeon and brought it into the prince's hands.

The prince said to it: "Tell me now, where are my brothers?" The pigeon replied: "I will; only do me no harm. Immediately behind your father's town is a water-mill, and in the water-mill are three wands that have sprouted up. Cut these three wands up from below, and strike with them upon their root; an iron door will immediately open into a large vault. In that vault are many people, old and young, rich and poor, small and great, wives and maidens, so that you could settle a populous empire; there, too, are your brothers." When the pigeon had told him all this, the prince immediately wrung its neck.

The emperor had gone out in person, and posted himself on the hill from which the grooms had viewed the shepherd, and he, too, was a spectator of all that had taken place. After the shepherd had thus obtained the dragon's head, twilight began to approach. He washed himself nicely, took the falcon on his shoulder, the hounds behind him, and the bagpipes under his arm, played as he went, drove the sheep, and proceeded to the emperor's palace, with the damsel at his side still in terror.

When they came to the town, all the town assembled as to see a wonder. The emperor, who had seen all his heroism from the hill, called him into his presence, and gave him his daughter, went immediately to church, had them married, and held a wedding festival for a week. After this the prince told him who and whence he was, and the emperor and the whole town rejoiced still more. Then, as the prince was urgent to go to his own home, the emperor gave him a large escort, and equipped him for the journey.

When they were in the neighbourhood of the water-mill, the prince halted his attendants, went inside, cut up the three wands, and struck the root with them, and the iron door opened at once. In the vault was a vast multitude of people. The prince ordered them to come out one by one, and go whither each would, and stood himself at the door. They came out thus one after another, and lo! there were his brothers also, whom he embraced and kissed. When the whole multitude had come out, they thanked him for releasing and delivering them, and went each to his own home. But he went to his father's house with his brothers and bride, and there lived and reigned to the end of his days.

—From *Sixty Folk-Tales from Exclusively Slavonic Sources* by Albert Henry Wratislaw, 1890. A similar version can be found in *The Crimson Fairy Book* by Andrew Lang, 1903.

—❖—

There was a piper had a cow,
And he had naught to give her;
He pulled out his pipes and played her a tune,
And bade the cow consider.
The cow considered very well,
And gave the piper a penny,
And bade him play the other tune,
"Corn rigs are bonny."
Traditional Nursery Rhyme

The Piper Came to Our Town

Great Hand and the Piper

In ancient days the dog was looked upon as man's best friend, and the enemy of all supernatural beings: fairies, giants, hags, and monsters of the sea and the Underworld. When the seasons changed on the four quarter days[1] of the year, and the whole world, as the folks believed, was thrown into confusion, the fairies and other spirits broke loose and went about plundering houses and barns and stealing children. At such times the dogs were watchful and active, and howled warning when they saw any of the supernatural creatures. They even attacked the fairies, and sometimes after such fights they returned home with all the hair scraped off their bodies.

A story is still current in Edinburgh about a piper and his dog, and their meeting with a monster of the Underworld. This monster haunted an underground passage, which is said to run from Edinburgh Castle to Holyrood Palace, and was called Great Hand, for no one ever saw aught of it except its gigantic grisly hand with nails like an eagle's claw.

In days of long ago the underground passage was used by soldiers when the enemies of the King of Scotland invaded the kingdom and laid siege to Edinburgh Castle, his chief stronghold. The soldiers could leave the castle and fall upon the besiegers from behind, and through it reinforcements could be sent to the castle. When, however, the spirit called Great Hand began to haunt the tunnel, it could not be used any longer, for every man who entered it perished in the darkness.

The piper was a brave man, and he resolved to explore the tunnel with his dog. "I shall play my bagpipe all the way through," he said to his friends, "and you can follow the sound of the piping above the ground."

There is a cave below the castle which leads to the tunnel, and

---

1. The equinoxes and solstices.

the piper entered it one morning, playing a merry tune. His faithful dog followed him. The people heard the sound of the bagpipe as they walked down High Street, listening intently, but when they reached the spot which is called the Heart of Midlothian[2] the piping stopped abruptly, as if the pipes had been torn suddenly from the piper's hands. The piper was never seen again, but his dog, without a hair on its body, came running out of the cave below the castle.

—Originally published as "Friends and Foes of Man" in *Wonder Tales from Scottish Myth and Legend* by Donald Alexander Mackenzie, 1917.

—❖—

How little is required for pleasure!
The sound of a bagpipe.
Without music, life would be an error.
Friedrich Nietzsche

---

2. A heart-shaped mosaic of granite stones on the pavement in front of St. Giles Cathedral marks the spot where the Old Tollbooth, which was the administrative center of Edinburgh, a prison, and one of several sites of public execution. According to Scottish tradition, it is good luck to spit into the heart.

The Piper Came to Our Town

The Russet Dog

Oh, he's a rare clever fellow, is the Russet Dog—the Fox, I suppose you call him. Have you ever heard the way he gets rid of his fleas? He hunts about and he hunts about till he finds a lock of wool; then he takes it in his mouth, and down he goes to the river and turns his tail to the stream, and goes in back-wards. And as the water comes up to his haunches the little fleas come forward, and the more he dips into the river the more they come forward, till at last he has got nothing but his snout and the lock of wool above water, then the little fleas rush into his snout and into the lock of wool. Down he dips his nose, and as soon as he feels his nose free of them, he lets go the lock of wool, and so he is free of his fleas.

Ah, but that is nothing to the way in which he catches ducks for his dinner. He will gather some heather, and put his head in the midst of it, and then will slip downstream to the place where the ducks are swimming, for all the world like a piece of floating heather. Then he lets go, and—gobble, gobble, gobble—till not a duck is left alive.

And he is as brave as he is clever. It's said that once he found the bagpipes lying all alone, and being very hungry began to gnaw at them; but as soon as he made a hole in the bag, out came a squeal. Was the Russet Dog afraid? Never a bit; all he said was: "Here's music with my dinner."

—From *More Celtic Fairy Tales* by Joseph Jacobs, 1894.

The Cow That Ate the Piper

The only introduction I shall attempt to the following "extravaganza" is to request the reader to suppose it to be delivered by a frolicking Irish peasant in the richest brogue and most dramatic manner:

"I'll tell you, sir, a mighty quare story, and it's as thrue as I'm standin' here, and that's no lie.

"It was in the time of the 'ruction[1], whin the long summer days, like many a fine fellow's precious life, was cut short by raison of the martial law, that wouldn't let a dacent boy be out in the evenin', good or bad; for whin the day's work was over, divil a one of us dar go to meet a frind over a glass, or a girl at the dance, but must go home and shut ourselves up, and never budge, nor rise latch, nor dhraw boult, antil the morning kem agin.

"Well, to come to my story. 'Twas afther night-fall, and we wor sittin' round the fire, and the praties wor boilin', and the noggins of butthermilk was standin' ready for our suppers, whin a knock kem to the door.

"'Whisht!' says my father. 'Here's the sojers come upon us now,' says he. 'Bad luck to thim, the villians! I'm afeared they seen a glimmer of the fire through the crack in the door,' says he.

"'No,' says my mother, 'for I'm afther hangin' an ould sack and my new petticoat agin it a while ago.'

"'Well, whisht, anyhow,' says my father, "for there's a knock agin,' and we all held our tongues till another thump kem to the door.

"'Oh, it's a folly to purtind any more,' says my father; 'they're too cute to be put off that-a-way,' says he. 'Go, Shamus,' says he to me, 'and see who's in it.'

"'How can I see who's in it in the dark?' says I.

"'Well,' says he, 'light the candle, thin, and see who's in it, but

---

1. Insurrection.

don't open the door, for your life, barrin' they brake it in,' says he, 'exceptin' to the sojers, and spake thim fair, if it's thim.'

"So with that I wint to the door, and there was another knock.

"'Who's there?' says I.

"'It's me,' says he.

"'Who are you?' says I.

"'A frind,' says he.

"'*Baithershin*!' says I, 'who are you, at all?'

"'Arrah! Don't you know me?' says he.

"'Divil a taste,' says I.

"'Sure I'm Paddy the Piper,' says he.

"'Oh, thunder an' turf,' says I, 'is it you, Paddy, that's in it?'

"'Sorra one else,' says he.

"'And what brought you at this hour?' says I.

"'By gar,' says he, 'I didn't like goin' the roun' by the road,' says he, 'and so I kem the short cut, and that's what delayed me,' says he.

"'Oh, bloody wars!' says I. 'Paddy, I wouldn't be in your shoes for the king's ransom,' says I; 'for you know yourself it's a hangin' matther to be cotched out these times,' says I.

"'Sure, I know that,' says he. 'God help me; and that's what I kem to you for,' says he; 'and let me in for ould acquaintance sake,' says poor Paddy.

"'Oh, by this and that,' says I, 'I darn't open the door for the wide world; and sure you know it; and throth, if the Husshians or the Yeos ketches you,' says I, 'they'll murther you, as sure as your name's Paddy.'

"'Many thanks to you,' says he, 'for your good intintions; but, plaze the pigs, I hope it's not the likes o' that is in store for me, anyhow.'

"'Faix, then,' says I, 'you had betther lose no time in hidin' yourself,' says I; 'for throth, I tell you, it's a short thrial and a long rope the Husshians would be afther givin' you—for they've no justice and less marcy, the villians!'

"'Faith, thin, more's the raison you should let me in, Shamus,' says poor Paddy.

"'It's a folly to talk,' says I. 'I darn't open the door.'

"'Oh, then, millia murther!' says Paddy, "what'll become of me, at all, at all?' says he.

"'Go aff into the shed,' says I, 'behin' the house, where the cow is, and there there's an iligant lock o' straw that you may go sleep in,' saya I, 'and a fine bed it id be for a lord, let alone a piper.'

"So off Paddy set to hide in the shed, and throth, it wint to our hearts to refuse him, and turn him away from the door, more by token when the praties was ready—for sure, the bit and the sup is always welkim to the poor thraveller. Well, we all wint to bed, and Paddy hid himself in the cow-house; and now I must tell you how it was with Paddy:

"You see, afther sleeping for some time, Paddy wakened up thinkin' it was mornin', but it wasn't mornin' at all, but only the light o' the moon that deceaved him; but at all evints, he wanted to be stirrin' airly, bekase he was goin' off to the town hard by, it bein' fair day, to pick up a few ha'pence with his pipes—for the divil a better piper was in all the counthry round nor Paddy; and everyone gave it up to Paddy that he was iligant an the pipes, and played 'Jinny bang'd the Weaver' beyant tellin', and the 'Hare in the Corn,' that you'd think the very dogs was in it and the horse-men ridin' like mad.

"Well, as I was sayin', he set off to go to the fair, and he wint meandherin' along through the fields, but he didn't go far, antil climbin' up through a hedge, when he was comin' out at t'other side, his head kem plump agin somethin' that made the fire flash out iv his eyes. So with that he looks up—and what do you think it was, Lord be merciful to us! but a corpse hangin' out of a branch of a three.

"'Oh, the top o' the mornin' to you, sir,' says Paddy, 'and is that the way with you, my poor fellow? Throth, you tuk a start out o' me,' says poor Paddy; and 'twas thrue for him, for it would make the heart of a stouter man nor Paddy jump to see the like, and to think of a Chrishthan crathur being hanged up, all as one as a dog.

"Now, 'twas the rebels that hanged this chap—bekase, you see, the corpse had got clothes an him, and that's the raison that one might know it was the rebels—by raison that the Husshians and the Orangemen never hanged anybody wid good clothes an him, but only the poor and definceless crathurs like us; so, as I said before, Paddy knew well it was the boys that done it; 'and,' says Paddy, eyin' the corpse, 'by my sowl, thin, but you have a beautiful pair o' boots an you,' says he, 'and it's what I'm thinkin' you won't have any great use for thim no more; and sure, it's a shame to the likes o' me,' says he, 'the best piper in the sivin counties, to be trampin' wid a pair of ould brogues not worth three *traneeens*, and a corpse with such an iligant pair o' boots, that wants someone to wear thim.' So, with that, Paddy lays hould of him by the boots, and began a-pullin' at thim, but they wor mighty stiff; and whether it wis by raison of their bein' so tight, or the branch of the three a-jiggin' up an' down, all as one as a weighdee buckettee, an' not lettin' Paddy cotch any right hoult o' thim—he could get no *advantage* o' thim at all—and at last he gev it up, and was goin' away, whin lookin' behind him agin, the sight of the iligant fine boots was too much for him, and he turned back, determined to have the boots, anyhow, by fair means or foul; and I'm loath to tell you now how he got thim—for indeed it was a dirty turn, and throth, it was the only dirty turn I ever knew Paddy to be guilty av; and you see it was this a-way; 'pon my sowl, he pulled out a big knife, and by the same token, it was a knife with a fine buckhandle and a murtherin' big blade, that an uncle o' mine, that was a gardener at the lord's, made Paddy a prisint av; and more by token, it was not the first mischief that knife done, for it cut love between thim, that was the best of finds before; and sure, 'twas the wondher of everyone, that two knowledgable men, that ought to know betther, would do the likes, and give and take sharp steel in frindship; but I'm forgettin'—well, he outs with his knife, and what does he do, but be cuts off the legs of the corpse; 'and,' says he, 'I can take off the boots at my convaynience;' and throth, it was, as I said before, a dirty turn.

"Well, Sir, he tuck'd the legs undher his arms, and at that minit the moon peeped out from behind a cloud— 'Oh! is it there you are?' says he to the moon, for he was an impidint chap—and thin, seein' that he made a mistake, and that the moonlight deceaved him, and that it wasn't the airly dawn, as he conceaved; and bein' friken'd for fear himself might be cotched and trated like the poor corpse he was afther a malthreating, if he was found walking the counthry at that time—by gar, he turned about, and walked back agin to the cow-house, and hidin' the corpse's legs in the sthraw, Paddy wint to sleep agin. But what do you think? The divil a long Paddy was there, antil the sojers came in airnest, and by the powers, they carried off Paddy—and faith, it was only sarvin' him right for what he done to the poor corpse.

"Well, whin the mornin' kem, my father says to me: 'Go, Shamus,' says he, 'to the shed, and bid poor Paddy come in, and take share o' the praties, for I go bail, he's ready for his breakquest by this, anyhow!'

"Well, out I wint to the cow-house, and called out 'Paddy!' and afther callin' three or four times, and gettin' no answer, I wint in, and called agin, and divil an answer I got still.

"'Blood-an-agers!' says I. 'Paddy, where are you, at all, at all?' And so, castin' my eyes about the shed, I seen two feet stickin' out from undher the hape o' straw— 'Musha! thin,' says I, 'bad luck to you, Paddy, but you're fond of a warm corner, and maybe you haven't made yourself as snug as a flay in a blanket? But I'll disturb your dhrames, I'm thinkin',' says I, and with that I laid hould of his heels (as I thought, God help me!), and givin' a good pull to waken him, as I intinded, away I wint, head over heels, and my brains was a'most knocked out agin' the wall.

"Well, whin I recovered myself, there I was, an the broad o' my back, and two things stickin' out o' my hands like a pair o' Husshian's horse-pist'ls—and I thought the sight 'id lave, my eyes when I seen they wor' two mortial legs.

"My jew'l, I threw them down like a hot pratie, and jumpin' up, I roared out millia murther. 'Oh, you murtherin' villian,' says I, shakin' my fist at the cow; 'oh, you unnath'ral *baste*,' says I, 'you've ate poor Paddy, you thievin' cannible; you're worse than a neygar,' says I; 'and bad luck to you, how dainty you are, that nothin' 'id serve you for your supper but the best piper in Ireland.

The Piper Came to Our Town

Weirasthru! Weirasthru! What'll the whole counthry say to such an unnath'ral murther? And you lookin' as innocent there as a lamb, and atin' your hay as quite as if nothin' happened.' With that I run out—for throth, I didn't like to be near her—and goin' into the house, I tould them all about it.

"'Arrah! Be aisy,' says my father.

"'Bad luck to the lie I tell you,' says I.

"'Is it ate Paddy?' says they.

"'Divil a doubt of it,' says I.

"'Are you sure, Shamus?' says my mother.

"'I wish I was as sure of a new pair o' brogues,' says I. 'Bad luck to the bit she has left iv him but his two legs.'

"'And do you tell me she ate the pipes too?' says my father.

"'By gor, I b'lieve so,' says I.

"'Oh, the divil fly away wid her,' says he. 'What a cruel taste she has for music!'

"'Arrah!' says my mother, 'don't be cursin' the cow that gives the milk to the childher.'

"'Yis, I will,' says my father. 'Why shouldn't I curse sich an unnath'ral baste?'

"'You oughtn't to curse any livin' thing that's undher your roof,' says my mother.

"'By my sowl, thin,' says my father, 'she shan't be undher my roof any more; for I'll sind her to the fair this minit,' says he, 'and sell her for whatever she'll bring. Go aff,' says he, 'Shamus, the minit you've ate your breakquest, and dhrive her to the fair.'

"'Throth, I don't like to dhrive her,' says I.

"'Arrah don't be makin' a gommagh of yourself,' says he.

"'Faith, I don't,' says I.

"'Well, like or no like,' says he, 'you must dhrive her.'

"'Sure, father,' says I, 'you could take more care iv her yourself.'

"'That's mighty good,' says he, 'to keep a dog and bark myself;' and faith, I rec'llected the sayin' from that hour. 'Let me have no more words about it,' says he, 'but be aff wid you.'

"So aff I wint—and it's no lie I'm tellin' whin I say it was sore agin my will I had anything to do with sich a villian of a baste.

But howsomever, I cut a brave long wattle, that I might dhrive the man-ather iv a thief, as she was, without bein' near her, at all, at all.

"Well, away we wint along the road, and mighty throng it wus wid the boys and the girls—and in short, all sorts, rich and poor, high and low, crowdin' to the fair.

"'God save you,' says one to me.

"'God save you, kindly,' says I.

"'That's a fine baste you're dhrivin',' says he.

"'Throth, she is,' says I; though God knows it wint agin my heart to say a good word for the likes of her.

"'It's to the fair you're goin', I suppose,' says he, 'with the baste?' (He was a snug-lookin' farmer, ridin' a purty little grey hack.)

"'Faith, thin, you're right enough,' says I, 'it is to the fair I'm goin'.'

"'What do you expec' for her?' says he.

"'Faith, thin, myself doesn't know,' says I—and that was thrue enough, you see, bekase I was bewildhered like about the baste entirely.

"'That's a quare way to be goin' to market,' says he; 'and not to know what you expec' for your baste.'

"'Och,' says I—not likin' to let him suspict there was anything wrong wid her— 'och,' says I, in a careless sort of a way, 'sure, no one can tell what a baste 'ill bring, antil they come to the fair,' says I, 'and see what price is goin'.'

"'Indeed, that's nath'ral enough,' says he. 'But if you wor bid a fair price before you come to the fair, sure you might as well take it,' says he.

"'Oh I've no objection in life,' says I.

"'Well, thin, what 'ill you ax for her?' says he.

"'Why, thin, I wouldn't like to be onraisonable,' says I—(for the thruth was, you know, I wanted to get rid iv her)—'and so I'll take four pounds for her,' says I, 'and no less.'

"'No less!' says he.

"'Why, sure, that's chape enough,' says I.

"'Throth; it is,' says he; 'and I'm thinkin' it's too chape it is,' says he; 'for if there wasn't somethin' the matter, it's not for that you'd be sellin' the fine milch cow, as she is to all appearance.'

"'Indeed, thin,' says I, 'upon my conscience, she is a fine milch cow.'

"'Maybe,' says he, 'she's gone off her milk, in regard that she doesn't feed well?'

"'Och, by this and that,' says I, 'in regard of feedin' there's not the likes of her in Ireland. So make your mind aisy; and if you like her for the money, you may have her.'

"'Why, indeed, I'm not in a hurry,' says he, 'and I'll wait to see how they go in the fair.'

"'With all my heart,' says I, purtendin' to be no ways consarned—but in throth, I began to be afeard that the people was seein' somethin' unnath'ral about her, and that we'd never get rid of her, at all, at all. At last we kem to the fair, and a great sight o' people was in it—throth, you'd think the whole world was there, let alone the standin's o' gingerbread and iligant ribbins, and makins o' beautiful gownds, and pitch-and-toss, and merry go-rouns, and tints with the best av dhrink in thim, and the fiddles playin' up t' incourage the boys and girls; but I never minded thim at all, but detarmint to sell the thievin' rogue av a cow afore I'd mind any divarsh in life; so an I dhriv her into the thick av the fair, whin all of a suddint, as I kem to the door av a tint, up sthruck the pipes to the tune av 'Tattherin' Jack Welsh,' and, my jew'l, in a minit the cow cock'd her ears, and was makin' a dart at the tint.

"'Oh, murther!' says I, to the boys standin' by, 'hould her,' says I, 'hould her—she ate one piper already, the vagabone, and bad luck to her, she wants another.'

"'Is it a cow for to ate a piper?' says one o' thim.

"'Divil a bit o' lie in it, for I seen his corpse myself, and nothin' left but the two legs,' says I; 'and it's a folly to be sthrivin' to hide it, for I see she'll never lave it aff—as poor Paddy Grogan knows to his cost, Lord be marciful to him!'

"'Who's that takin' my name in vain?' says a voice in the crowd; and with that, shovin' the throng a one side, who the divil should I see but Paddy Grogan, to all appearance.

"'Oh, hould him too,' says I. 'Keep him av me, for it's not himself at all, but his ghost,' says I; 'for he was kilt last night to my sartin knowledge, every inch av him, all to his legs.'

"Well, sir, with that, Paddy—for it was Paddy himself, as it kem out afther—fell a laughin', that you'd think his sides 'ud split; and whin he kem to himself, he ups and he tould us howit was, as I tould you already; and the likes av the fun they made av me was beyant tellin' for wrongfully misdoubtin' the poor cow, and layin' the blame iv atin' a piper an her. So we all wint into a tint to have it explained, and by gor, it tuk a full gallon o' sper'ts t' explain it; and we dhrank health and long life to Paddy and the cow, and Paddy played that day beyant all tellin', and many a one said the likes was never heerd before or sence, even from Paddy himself—and av coorse, the poor slandhered cow was dhruv home agin, and many a quite day she had wid us afther that; and whin she died, throth, my father had sitch a regard for the poor thing, that he had her skinned, and an iligant pair of breeches made out iv her hide, and it's in the fam'ly to this day; and isn't it mighty remarkable it is, what I'm goin' to tell you now, but it's as thrue as I'm here, and from that out, anyone that has them breeches an, the minit a pair o' pipes sthrikes up, they can't rest, but goes jiggin' and jiggin' in their sate, and never stops as long as the pipes is playin'—and there," said he, slapping the garment in question that covered his sinewy limb, with a spank of his brawny hand that might have startled nerves more tender than mine—"there, there is the very breeches that's an me now and a fine pair they are this minit."

—From *Legends and Stories of Ireland* by Samuel Lover, 1831. Originally titled "Paddy the Piper."

The Piper Came to Our Town

The Cow That Ate the Piper

In the year ninety-eight, when our troubles were great,
    And it was treason to be a Milesian.
That black-whiskered set we will never forget,
    Though history tells us they were Hessians.
In this troublesome time, oh! twas a great crime,
    And murder never was riper,
At the side of Glenshee, not an acre from me,
    There lived one Denny Byrne, a piper.

Neither wedding or wake would be worth a shake,
    Where Denny was not first invited,
At squeezing the bags and emptying the kegs,
    He astonished as well as delighted.
In these times poor Denny could not earn one penny,
    Martial law had him stung like a viper;
They kept him within till the bones and the skin
    Were grinning thro' the rags of the piper.

One evening in June, as he was going home,
    After the fair of Rathnagan.
What should he see from the branch of a tree,
    But the corpse of a Hessian there hanging.
Says Denny, "These rogues have boots, I've brogues,"
    On the boots then he laid such a griper,
He pulled with such might, and the boots were so tight,
    That legs and boots came away with the piper.

Then Denny did run, for fear of being hung,
    Till he came to Tim Kennedy's cabin;
Says Tim from within, "I can't let you in,
    You'll be shot if you're caught there a-rappin'."
He went round to the shed, where the cow was in bed,
    With a wisp he began to wipe her—

They lay down together on a seven-foot feather;
    And the cow fell a-hugging the piper.

Then Denny did yawn, as the day it did dawn,
    And he streel'd off the boots of the Hessian;
The legs—by the law! he left on the straw,
    And he gave them leg-bail for his mission.
When the breakfast was done, Tim sent out his son
    To make Denny jump up like a lamplighter;
When the legs there he saw, he roar'd like a jackdaw,
    "Oh, daddy! the cow's ate the piper."

"Musha bad luck on the beast—she'd a musical taste,
    For to eat such a beautiful chanter,
Arrah! Patrick avic, take a lump of a stick,
    Drive her off to Glenhealy—we'll cant her."
Mrs. Kennedy bawl'd, and the neighbors were call'd,
    They began for to humbug and gibe her;
To the churchyard Tim walked, with the legs in a box,
    And the cow will be hung for the piper.

The cow she was drove a mile or two off,
    To the fair at the side of Glenhealy,
And there she was sold for four guineas in gold
    To the clerk of the parish, Tim Daly.
They went to a tent, the luck-penny was spent,
    The clerk being a jolly old swiper,
Who d'ye think was there, playing the "Rakes of Kildare,"
    But poor Denny Byrne, the piper!

Then Tim gave a bolt, like a half-drunken colt,
    At the piper he gazed like a gommach;
He said: "By the powers! I thought these eight hours
    You were playing in driman dhu's stomach!"
Then Denny observed how the Hessian was served,
    So they all wish'd Nick's cure to the griper;

                                    The Piper Came to Our Town

For grandeur they met, their whistles they wet,
  And like fairies they danced round the piper.

—From *Irish Com-All-Ye's* by Manus O'Conor, 1901.

— ❖ —

The Pipers

Fhairshon swore a feud
  Against the clan M'Tavish—
March'd into their land
  To murder and to rafish;
For he did resolve,
  To extirpate ta vipers,
With four-and-twenty men
  And five-and-thirty pipers.

—Excerpt from "Massacre of the MacPherson,"
A Victorian Anthology, 1837–1895, edited by
Edmund Clarence Stedman, 1897.

— ❖ —

*A baggepipe wel koude he blowe and sowne
And therwithal he broughte us out of towne.*
**Prologue: The Miller, from *Canterbury Tales*,
Geoffrey Chaucer**

The Cattle Jobber
of Awnascawil

There was a cattle jobber once who was going to a fair near Awnascawil, and he met the good people [fairies] about nightfall on the way. They took him with them and turned from the road into a lonely field in which was a large fairy fort. When they went in he saw a house as grand as any he had ever put foot in. The company ate and drank enough, and the good people pressed him to sit at the table, but he would taste neither food nor drink.

Next morning after breakfast they went out, leaving no one behind but their piper, whose name was Tim.

"You are not to let that man out of this while we are gone," said they to the piper.

The jobber noticed that when they were going, every one of the fairies dipped his finger in a box that hung by the door and rubbed his eyes. When the jobber thought that they were off a good distance he said to himself: "I'm man enough for this piper." With that he began to lace his shoes and prepare for his journey.

"What are you doing?" asked the piper.

"I'm going to be off out o' this," said the jobber. "I think it long enough that I'm here."

"You'll not leave this while I am in it," said the piper. "You heard the order to keep you here till they came back."

"Indeed then you'll not keep me, and I won't stay with you." With that he rose, and no sooner was he on his feet than the piper caught him and they went at each other.

In the wrestling the jobber knocked Tim across a tub that was standing on the floor and broke his back. The piper didn't stir after that: how could he and his back broken. With that the jobber sprang to the door, put his finger in the box and rubbed one eye with the finger in the same way that he saw the fairies doing, and when his eye was rubbed he could see all the fairies in the world with that eye if they were before him, and not a one could he see with the other eye. He set forward then, spent one night on the road, and as the fair was to be held on the following day he stopped in a house not far from the fair ground. The day was close and warm and the jobber was thirsty, so he asked for a drink of water.

"You'll get it and welcome," said the woman of the house, "and it isn't water I'd give you to drink, but milk, if I could go for it, but I can't leave the cradle as something is the matter with the child since yesterday; neither I nor my husband slept a wink last night from taking care of him, and he screeching always."

"Well," said the jobber, "I'll take care of the cradle while you are after the milk, and sure the child will not die during that time."

The woman went for the milk, and the jobber rocked the cradle. He noticed that the screeching was different from the crying of a child, and caught hold of the blanket to take it from the child's face; but, if he did, the child had a firm grip of the clothes, and the jobber had to tear away the blanket. When he had the blanket away he saw what was in the cradle, and what was it, sure enough, but Tim the Piper. The man and his wife were young people, and the child was their firstborn.

"What brought you here, you scoundrel?" asked the jobber.

"Oh, when you broke my back," said Tim, "I could do nothing for the good people; they had no further use for me in the fort, so they put me here and took the child of the house with them."

"If you are here itself, why can't you hold your tongue and not be destroying the people with your screeching? Sure this is a good place you are in."

"Oh," said the piper, "I wouldn't cry, but for the rocking; it's the rocking that's killing me. It was you that broke my back, and don't expose me now."

"I'll expose you this minute," said the jobber, "unless you stop quiet."

"I'll stop quiet," said the piper.

When the woman came back the child was not crying. "What did you do to quiet him?" asked she.

"I only uncovered his face, and said that I'd kill him if he didn't stop quiet, and I suppose the child is in dread, as I am a stranger."

"You might as well stay the night with us," said the woman.

The jobber agreed, and as the child was quiet the mother could look to her work. When her husband came home in the evening she told him that the child had stopped crying since the stranger came, and the husband was glad.

"As the child is peaceable," said the jobber to the mother, "I'll take care of him to-night; you can go to bed."

The parents went to bed and left the child with their guest. About midnight the man saw that he was growing sleepy, and he pushed Tim and asked, "Couldn't you play a tune that would keep me awake?"

"It would be hard for me to play and my back broken," said Tim, "but if I had the pipes and you'd prop me in the cradle I might play."

"Where are the pipes?"

"My pipes were brought here," said Tim; "they are on the corner of the loft above the fireplace."

The jobber rose up, took the pipes, and fitted them together. The piper began to play, and his music was so sweet that it could raise the dead out of the grave. He was not long playing when the father and mother heard the music, and they had never heard the like of it.

"Who is the piper?" asked the man.

"I am," said the jobber; "when I am on the road I play often to amuse myself."

Tim threw away the pipes then, stretched back, and stopped quiet till morning. The father and mother were glad that their child was resting. After breakfast the jobber asked the mother had they good turf, and she said they had. "Bring in two or three creels of it," said he.

She brought the turf, and he put it down on the fire. When the fire was blazing well the mother was outside. Said the jobber to Tim: "You were a bad host when I met you last, and you'll not be here any longer; I'll burn you now."

He went to the door then to call the mother. He wanted her to see what would happen, and not finding her he came back to the cradle, but found nothing in it except the clothes. Then he got terribly afraid that he would be brought to account for the child.

The mother came in and asked: "Where is my child?"

He told her everything. He and the woman went to the door to search for the piper, and what should the woman see outside the door but her own child. She was very glad then. The jobber gave her good-bye and started for the fair. On the way he felt a great storm of wind and hail coming towards him, and stooped down for shelter under a bush at the side of a ditch. When the storm was passing he saw that it was a legion of fairies destroying everything before them, tearing up potato stalks and all that stood in their way.

"Oh, shame!" cried the jobber, "to be ruining poor people's labour."

A slender, foxy, red-haired man, a fairy, turned towards him, and, putting his finger into the jobber's eye, took the sight from him. Never again did he see a fairy. When the foxy fairy went back to the [horde of fairies] he asked: "Did ye see that man who was with us in the fort, the man who broke the back of Tim the Piper, and did ye hear what he said?"

"We did not."

"Well, I saw him and heard him. I took the sight from him; he'll never see one of us again."

The jobber went to the fair, though he had but the one eye.

—From *Tales of the Fairies and of the Ghost World* by Jeremiah Curtin, 1895.

The Host of the Air

O'Driscoll drove with a song,
The wild duck and the drake,
From the tall and the tufted reeds
Of the drear Hart Lake.

And he saw how the reeds grew dark
At the coming of night tide,
And dreamed of the long dim hair
Of Bridget his bride.

He heard while he sang and dreamed
A piper piping away,
And never was piping so sad,
And never was piping so gay.

And he saw young men and young girls
Who danced on a level place
And Bridget his bride among them,
With a sad and a gay face.

The dancers crowded about him,
And many a sweet thing said,
And a young man brought him red wine
And a young girl white bread.

But Bridget drew him by the sleeve,
Away from the merry bands,
To old men playing at cards
With a twinkling of ancient hands.

The bread and the wine had a doom,
For these were the host of the air;
He sat and played in a dream
Of her long dim hair.

He played with the merry old men
And thought not of evil chance,
Until one bore Bridget his bride
Away from the merry dance.

He bore her away in his arms,
The handsomest young man there,
And his neck and his breast and his arms
Were drowned in her long dim hair.

O'Driscoll scattered the cards
And out of his dream awoke:
Old men and young men and young girls
Were gone like a drifting smoke;

But he heard high up in the air
A piper piping away,
And never was piping so sad,
And never was piping so gay.

—From *The Poetical Works of William Butler Yeats,* vol. 1, 1911.

—❖—

Cherries of the night are riper
Than the cherries pluckt at noon,
Gather to your fairy piper
When he pipes his magic tune.
Robert Graves, "Cherry Time"

The Piper Came to Our Town

The Fairy Pipes

The old grandfather sat over the fire at the hour of sunset with his little grandson between his knees, and told to the little one the tale which I now tell to you.

Once, long ago, before the Sassanach with his dreary tongue came among us, there lived a man of our clan, who, in the days of his youth, had followed the fairy piper. To this day is the story told by many an evening fire, and many are those who listen on the hills for the sound of the magic pipes, which sounded as if they were made of gold of the purest, so sweet, so sad, so long drawn-out, were the strains which the fairy piper drew from them.

One day, when Ian, son of Seumas, was tending the flocks on the hill side, he was roused by the sound of pipe-music, which seemed to come from far, far away over the mountains. No mortal piper ever raised such strains, and when Ian heard them, unconsciously his feet led him, as he thought, nearer and nearer the direction from whence the haunting melodies came. Over hill, over dale, beside mighty rivers, by the shores of dark lochs—on and on he went, and it seemed to him that it was but a day that he travelled. But it was many days ere his people saw his face again.

On and on, led ever by music so sweet that not even a MacCrimmon of Skye ever raised such, so that once heard by mortal man must haunt his dreams for ever, he walked, and ever it seemed that when he quickened his steps the piper quickened his also, for never a sign of him did he see.

Though he little knew it, the days were slipping into weeks, and the weeks into months, and still he seemed to have lost all count of time. He lived on the scanty fare which the berries and roots afforded, with now and then a meal snatched hastily at some farm house. And strange it was, but it was as if the piper halted when he halted, and, when he again took to the road, the weird, sweet strains of the pipes reached him from a distance no farther off and no nearer than when he stopped to rest. And so it was when he slept; when he awoke the music was always sounding at the same distance as when he fell asleep.

And many were the dawns which rose in the East and flushed the sky with a flush rosy as that on the face of a maiden when her lover nears her; many were the sunsets which glowed in the West, the cloud-islands seeming to him like the islands of the blest, the "Tir nan Oig" of his dreams, as the radiant colours grew and faded. Rose and purple and amethyst, crimson, greens like the green of the fairy queen's robe, scarlet and topaz. And still, on and on, on and on, the fairy piper led him by the music of his golden-mouthed pipes.

So it was, that spring had passed into summer, summer into autumn, and autumn into winter, and winter into spring again, and still Ian the son of Seumas knew it not. If he could have had his choice whether he would live this music-haunted life or that old one which by now was as a dream to him, you may be sure that he would have chosen this one which he now led. For the dreamer has the best of it, and there is no dreamer like the man of the mountains, the Celt whose heritage is a heritage of the dreams and visions of the poets and seers.

Many and sweet and strange were the dreams and visions which were the lot of Ian the son of Seumas at that time; and when once a man has tasted of such glamour, the things of earth are never so near or so much to him for ever afterwards. His eyes are opened to the inward things; the glory of sea and mountain, river, glen, and song of bird, are seen and heard by him with eyes and ears which have been anointed with that which has made his seeing and hearing as the seeing and hearing of those who know and understand. The sound of the wind as it sighs and moans in the forests is never just the sighing of the wind to him again; but now he hears and knows that which it is only given to the few to hear and know, what the wind says, and what are the spirits of the wind.

And many were the storms which he encountered on that strange journey of his. For a night and a day towards the end of his wanderings there was a heavy storm, and, after it had passed, leaving a calm, cool evening, it seemed to Ian that now, at last, the fairy piper was almost within hail, so close did the sound of the pipes seem to be to him. So he followed their notes in the calm of that still evening-time, and at last he was led down to the shore of a sea-loch just as the moon was rising. And a voice spoke to him in accents so sweet and weird, that Ian said afterwards that the chill he felt then to the very marrow of his bones, when those unearthly tones fell upon his ear, was as the chill the man feels who loses his way in the enow.

And now the pipes were silent; only the echoes of their wonderful music rang in his ears. Neither piper nor pipes were to be seen, only the tones of that clear, sweet voice reached the ear of the wanderer. The voice bade him follow to the edge of the waves, and there, rocking on the tiny wavelets, on the golden path cast by the now risen moon, was a boat of silver. Obeying a command to enter the boat, he was rowed by unseen hands across the pathway cast by the rays of the moon, until the farther shore was reached.

As he stepped ashore it seemed to him that his eyes were touched by invisible fingers, and that which before had been hidden to his human sight now became clear to him. A young man stood before him clad in the fairy green—a green like the green of the first spring grass on the mountains—and shimmering as the grass does when the dew-drops bespangle it in the early morning. Under his arm he carried the most wonderful set of pipes that Ian had ever seen—green and gold and silver, the fairy pipes — whose music was as the music heard in dreams. "Come with me, Ian, son of Seumas, come with me where you will be welcome, and will need no more trouble about the things that grieve the sons of men," and, taking him by the hand, he led him to the face of a cliff. As they neared this cliff a door opened in it, and there was revealed such a scene of beauty as dazzled his eyes. A crystal hall with pillars of silver and gold stretched under the rock, and the radiance that gleamed from within was as the radiance of the moonshine on the sea. Fearing greatly, for the first time he failed to follow his guide, loosening his hold of the fairy man's hand. Then in gentlest

The Piper Came to Our Town

and kindest and sweetest tones the fairy told of the wonders to be seen and known by him if only he would accept the love of a fairy maiden who had seen and loved him as he watched his sheep on the side of the Ben now so far away. But ever after, Ian son of Seumas, said when telling the tale of this strange happening, that at that moment a new strength to resist temptation came to him; so, muttering a prayer (and all the time of his wanderings he had forgotten how to pray), he covered his eyes with his hands and fled—far, far, running as if possessed—and on the night air weird voices and music and singing were borne to him.

But the sound of the fairy pipes was heard by him no longer, and after many weeks he again reached the sheiling in the glen, a weary, haggard man, with unshorn hair and beard, so weak and forlorn, with his clothes in rags, that he was treated as a stranger beggar until his old mother saw him, who opened her arms and took the wanderer's head upon her bosom.

So he came to his own people once more, and married a daughter of the clan, and sometimes, when pressed, he would go over the strange tale of the fairy piper and his fairy pipes. But until the day of his death, Ian the son of Seumas would at times become unconscious of all around him, and walk as a man in a dream, and the wise woman of the village said that at such times he saw that which but few mortals are given to see.

So he lived and died in his own place, and the wise woman said that at his burial she heard the fairy pipes come sounding from far over the mountains, and that the tune they played was one which no earthly piper could ever essay. And that, little one, is the tale of the "Fairy Pipes."

—by Margaret T. Macgregor, from *The Celtic Monthly: A Magazine for Highlanders*, Vol. XIII, edited by John MacKay, 1905.

Hans the Hedgehog

There was once a countryman who had money and land in plenty, but how rich soever he was, one thing was still wanting in his happiness—he had no children. Often when he went into the town with the other peasants they mocked him and asked why he had no children. At last he became angry, and when he got home he said, "I will have a child, even if it be a hedgehog." Then his wife had a child that was a hedgehog in the upper part of his body, and a boy in the lower, and when she saw the child, she was terrified, and said, "See, there, thou hast brought ill-luck on us." Then said the man, "What can be done now? The boy must be christened, but we shall not be able to get a godfather for him." The woman said, "And we cannot call him anything else but Hans the Hedgehog."

When he was christened, the parson said, "He cannot go into any ordinary bed because of his spikes." So a little straw was put behind the stove, and Hans the Hedgehog was laid on it. His mother could not suckle him, for he would have pricked her with his quills. So he lay there behind the stove for eight years, and his father was tired of him and thought, "If he would but die!" He did not die, however, but remained lying there.

Now it happened that there was a fair in the town, and the peasant was about to go to it, and asked his wife what he should bring back with him for her. "A little meat and a couple of white rolls which are wanted for the house," said she. Then he asked the servant, and she wanted a pair of slippers and some stockings with clocks. At last he said also, "And what wilt thou have, Hans my Hedgehog?" "Dear father," he said, "do bring me bagpipes." When, therefore, the father came home again, he gave his wife what he had bought for her, meat and white rolls; and then he gave the maid the slippers and the stockings with clocks; and, lastly, he went behind the stove, and gave Hans the Hedgehog the bagpipes. And when Hans the Hedgehog had the bagpipes, he said, "Dear father, do go to the forge and get the cock shod, and then I will ride away, and never come back again."

On this, the father was delighted to think that he was going to get rid of him, and had the cock shod for him, and when it was done, Hans the Hedgehog got on it, and rode away, but took swine and asses with him which he intended to keep in the forest. When they got there he made the cock fly on to a high tree with him, and there he sat for many a long year, and watched his asses and swine until the herd was quite large, and his father knew nothing about him.

While he was sitting in the tree, however, he played his bagpipes, and made music which was very beautiful. Once a King came travelling by who had lost his way and heard the music. He was astonished at it, and sent his servant forth to look all round and see from whence this music came. He spied about, but saw nothing but a little animal sitting up aloft on the tree, which looked like a cock with a hedgehog on it which made this music. Then the King told the servant he was to ask why he sat there, and if he knew the road which led to his kingdom. So Hans the Hedgehog descended from the tree, and said he would show the way if the King would write a bond and promise him whatever he first met in the royal courtyard as soon as he arrived at home. Then the King thought, "I can easily do that, Hans the Hedgehog understands nothing, and I can write what I like."

So the King took pen and ink and wrote something, and when he had done it, Hans the Hedgehog showed him the way, and he got safely home. But his daughter, when she saw him from afar, was so overjoyed that she ran to meet him, and kissed him. Then he remembered Hans the Hedgehog, and told her what had happened, and that he had been forced to promise whatsoever first met him when he got home, to a very strange animal which sat on a cock as if it were a horse, and made beautiful music, but that instead of writing that he should have what he wanted, he had written that he should not have it. Thereupon the princess was glad, and said he had done well, for she never would have gone away with the Hedgehog.

Hans the Hedgehog, however, looked after his asses and pigs, and was always merry and sat on the tree and played his bag-pipes.

Now it came to pass that another King came journeying by with his attendants and runners, and he also had lost his way, and did not know how to get home again because the forest was so large. He likewise heard the beautiful music from a distance, and asked his runner what that could be, and told him to go and see. Then the runner went under the tree, and saw the cock sitting at the top of it, and Hans the Hedgehog on the cock. The runner asked him what he was about up there? "I am keeping my asses and my pigs; but what is your desire?" The messenger said that they had lost their way, and could not get back into their own kingdom, and asked if he would not show them the way. Then Hans the Hedgehog got down the tree with the cock, and told the aged King that he would show him the way, if he would give him for his own whatsoever first met him in front of his royal palace. The King said, "Yes," and wrote a promise to Hans the Hedgehog that he should have this. That done, Hans rode on before him on the cock, and pointed out the way, and the King reached his kingdom again in safety.

When he got to the courtyard, there were great rejoicings. Now he had an only daughter who was very beautiful; she ran to meet him, threw her arms round his neck, and was delighted to have her old father back again. She asked him where in the world he had been so long. So he told her how he had lost his way, and had very nearly not come back at all, but that as he was travelling through a great forest, a creature, half hedgehog, half man, who was sitting astride a cock in a high tree, and making music, had shown him the way and helped him to get out, but that in return he had promised him whatsoever first met him in the royal court-yard, and how that was she herself, which made him unhappy now. But on this she promised that, for love of her father, she would willingly go with this Hans if he came.

Hans the Hedgehog, however, took care of his pigs, and the

pigs multiplied until they became so many in number that the whole forest was filled with them. Then Hans the Hedgehog resolved not to live in the forest any longer, and sent word to his father to have every stye in the village emptied, for he was coming with such a great herd that all might kill who wished to do so. When his father heard that, he was troubled, for he thought Hans the Hedgehog had died long ago. Hans the Hedgehog, however, seated himself on the cock, and drove the pigs before him into the village, and ordered the slaughter to begin. Ha! but there was a killing and a chopping that might have been heard two miles off! After this Hans the Hedgehog said, "Father, let me have the cock shod once more at the forge, and then I will ride away and never come back as long as I live." Then the father had the cock shod once more, and was pleased that Hans the Hedgehog would never return again.

Hans the Hedgehog rode away to the first kingdom. There the King had commanded that whosoever came mounted on a cock and had bagpipes with him should be shot at, cut down, or stabbed by everyone, so that he might not enter the palace. When, therefore, Hans the Hedgehog came riding thither, they all pressed forward against him with their pikes, but he spurred the cock and it flew up over the gate in front of the King's window and lighted there, and Hans cried that the King must give him what he had promised, or he would take both his life and his daughter's. Then the King began to speak his daughter fair, and to beg her to go away with Hans in order to save her own life and her father's. So she dressed herself in white, and her father gave her a carriage with six horses and magnificent attendants together with gold and possessions. She seated herself in the carriage, and placed Hans the Hedgehog beside her with the cock and the bagpipes, and then they took leave and drove away, and the King thought he should never see her again.

He was however, deceived in his expectation, for when they were at a short distance from the town, Hans the Hedgehog took her pretty clothes off, and pierced her with his hedgehog's skin until she bled all over. "That is the reward of your falseness," said he. "Go your way, I will not have you!" and on that he chased her home again, and she was disgraced for the rest of her life.

Hans the Hedgehog, however, rode on further on the cock, with his bagpipes, to the dominions of the second King to whom he had shown the way. This one, however, had arranged that if any one resembling Hans the Hedgehog should come, they were to present arms, give him safe conduct, cry long life to him, and lead him to the royal palace.

But when the King's daughter saw him she was terrified, for he looked quite too strange. She remembered, however, that she could not change her mind, for she had given her promise to her father. So Hans the Hedgehog was welcomed by her, and married to her, and had to go with her to the royal table, and she seated herself by his side, and they ate and drank. When the evening came and they wanted to go to sleep, she was afraid of his quills, but he told her she was not to fear, for no harm would befall her, and he told the old King that he was to appoint four men to watch by the door of the chamber, and light a great fire, and when he entered the room and was about to get into bed, he would creep out of his hedgehog's skin and leave it lying there by the bedside, and that the men were to run nimbly to it, throw it in the fire, and stay by it until it was consumed.

When the clock struck eleven, he went into the chamber, stripped off the hedgehog's skin, and left it lying by the bed. Then came the men and fetched it swiftly, and threw it in the fire; and when the fire had consumed it, he was delivered, and lay there in bed in human form, but he was coal-black as if he had been burnt. The King sent for his physician who washed him with precious salves, and anointed him, and he became white, and was a handsome young man. When the King's daughter saw that she was glad, and the next morning they arose joyfully, ate and drank, and then the marriage was properly solemnized, and Hans the Hedgehog received the kingdom from the aged King.

When several years had passed he went with his wife to his father, and said that he was his son. The father, however, declared he had no son, he had never had but one, and he had been born like a hedgehog with spikes, and had gone forth into the world. Then Hans made himself known, and the old father rejoiced and went with him to his kingdom.

My tale is done,
And away it has run
To little August's house.

—From *Household Tales by Jacob and Wilhelm Grimm*, translated by Margaret Hunt, 1884.

—❖—

Now Felix Magee puts his pipes to his knee,
And with a flourish so free sets each couple in motion;
With a cheer and a bound the lads patter the ground;
The maids move around, just like swans on the ocean.
From the traditional song "Kitty Neil"

The Caraiman

The Caraiman[1] towers up, dark and threatening of aspect, with his mighty peak of rock, that looks as though a great fragment of it had been partly loosened, and were hanging in mid-air. That part of the rock is shaped like a set of bagpipes—and this is the tale they tell about it.

Long, long, ago, when the sky was nearer to the earth than now, and there was more water than land, there dwelt a mighty sorcerer in the Carpathians. He was as tall as the tallest pine-tree, and he carried upon his head a whole tree with green twigs and budding branches. His beard, that was many yards long, was of moss, and so were his eyebrows. His clothing was of bark, his voice was like rolling thunder, and beneath his arm he carried a set of bagpipes as big as a house. He could do anything he liked with his bagpipes. When he played softly, young green sprang up all round about him, as far as his eye could reach; if he blew harder, he could create living things; but when he blew fearfully loud, then such a storm arose that the mountains shook and the sea shrank back from the rocks, so that more land was left uncovered.

Once he was attacked by some powerful enemies, but instead of having to defend himself, he merely put the bagpipes to his lips, and changed his foes into pines and beech-trees. He was never tired of playing, for it delighted his ear when the echo sent back the sound of his music to him, but still more was his eye delighted to see all grow into life around him. Then would thousands of sheep appear on every height and from every valley, and upon the forehead of each grew a little tree, whereby the Caraiman might know which were his; and from the stones around, too, dogs sprang forth, and every one of them knew his voice. Since he had not noticed much that was good in the inhabitants of other coun-

---

1. The Caraiman is a mountain peak located in Romania, in the Bucegi Mountains of the Southern Carpathians.

tries, he hesitated a long while before making any human beings. Yet he came to the conclusion that children were good and loving, and he decided to people his land with children only. So he began to play the sweetest tune he had ever yet composed—and behold! children sprang up on every side, and yet more children, in endless crowds. Now you can fancy how wonderful the Caraiman's kingdom looked. Nothing but play was ever carried on there; and the little creatures toddled and rolled around in that beautiful world and were very happy. They crept under the ewes and sucked the milk from their udders; they plucked herbs and fruit and ate them; they slept on beds of moss and under overhanging rocks, and were as happy as the day was long. Their happiness crept even into their sleep, for then the Caraiman played them the loveliest airs, so that they had always beautiful dreams.

There was never any angry word spoken in the kingdom of the Caraiman, for these children were all so sweet and joyful that they never quarreled with one another. There was no occasion for envy or jealousy, either, since each one's lot was as happy as his neighbor's, and the Caraiman took care that there should be plenty of sheep to feed the children; and with his music he always provided enough of grass and herbs, that the sheep, too, might be well nourished.

No child ever hurt itself, either; the dogs took care of that, for they carried them about and sought out the softest, mossiest spots for their playgrounds. If a child fell into the water, the dogs fetched it out; and if one were tired, a dog would take it upon his back and carry it into the cool shade to rest. In short, the children were as happy as though they had been in Paradise. They never wished for anything more, since they had never seen anything outside their little world.

There were not yet any "smart" or "ugly" clothes then, nor any fine palaces with miserable huts beside them, so that no one could look enviously at his neighbor's belongings. Sickness and death were unknown, too, in the Caraiman's country, for the creatures he made came into the world as perfect as a chick from its shell, and there was no need for any to die, since there was so much room for all. All the land which he had redeemed from the sea had to be populated, and for nothing but sheep and children there was room on it, and to spare, for many a long day.

The children knew nothing of reading or writing; it was not necessary that they should, since everything came to them of itself, and they had to take no trouble about anything. Neither did they need any further knowledge, since they were exposed to no dangers.

Yet, as they grew older, they learned to dig out little dwellings for themselves in the ground and to carpet them with moss, and then of a sudden they began to say, "This is mine."

But when once a child had begun to say, "This is mine," all the others wanted to say it too. Some built themselves huts like the first; but others found it much easier to nestle into those that were already made, and then, when the owners cried and complained, the unkind little conquerors laughed. Thereupon those who had been cheated of their belongings struck out with their fists, and so the first battle arose. Some ran and brought complaints to the Caraiman, who in consequence blew a mighty thunder upon his bagpipes, which frightened all the children terribly.

So they learned for the first time to know fear; and afterward they showed anger against the tale-bearers. In this way even strife and division entered into the Caraiman's beautiful, peaceful kingdom.

He was deeply grieved when he saw how the tiny folk in his kingdom behaved in just the same way as the grown people in other lands, and he debated how he might cure the evil. Should he blow them all away into the sea, and make a new family? But the new ones would soon be as bad as these, and then, he was really too fond of his little people. Next he thought of taking away everything over which they might quarrel; but then all would become dry and barren, for it was but over a handful of earth and moss that the strife had arisen, and, in truth, only because some of the children had been industrious, and others lazy. Then he bethought himself of making them presents, and gave to each sheep and dogs and a garden for his particular use. But this only made

The Piper Came to Our Town

things far worse. Some planted their gardens, but others let them run wild, and then perceived that the cultivated gardens were the fairest, and that the sheep that had good pasture gave the most milk. Then the trouble became great indeed. The lazy children made a league against the others, attacked them, and took away many of their gardens. Then the industrious ones moved to a fresh spot, which soon grew fair also under their hands; or else they refused to be driven out, and long conflicts arose, in the course of which some of the children were slain. When they saw death for the first time, they were greatly frightened and grieved, and swore to keep peace with one another. But all in vain—they could not stay quiet for long; so, as they were now loath to kill one another, they began to take away each other's property by stealth and with cunning. And this was far sadder to see. The Caraiman, indeed, grew so heavy of heart over it that he wept rivers of tears. They flowed down through the valley and into the sea; yet the wicked children never considered that these were the tears their kind father was weeping over them, and went on bickering and quarreling.

Thereupon the Caraiman wept ever more and more, and his tears turned to torrents and cataracts that devastated the land, and ended by changing it into one large lake, wherein countless living creatures came to their death. Then he ceased weeping, and blew a mighty wind, which left the land dry again. But now all the green growth had vanished; houses and gardens lay buried under heaps of stones; and the sheep, for lack of pasture, no longer gave any milk; then the children cut the sheeps' throats open with sharp stones, to see if the milk would not flow out in a fresh place; but instead of milk, blood gushed out, and when they had drunk that they became fierce, and were always craving more of it. So they slew many other sheep, stealing those of their brethren, and drank blood and ate meat. Then the Caraiman said, "There must me larger animals made, or there will soon be none left," and blew again upon his bagpipes. And behold! wild bulls came into the world, and winged horses with long scaly tails, and elephants, and serpents. The children now began to fight with all these creatures, and thereby grew very tall and strong themselves. Many of the animals allowed themselves to be tamed and made useful, but others pursued the children and killed them; and as they no longer dwelt in such peace and safety, many grievous and dangerous sicknesses appeared among them. Soon they became in all respects like the men of other lands, and the Caraiman grew more and more soured and gloomy, since all that which he had intended to use for good had but turned to evil. His creatures, too, neither loved nor trusted him, and, instead of perceiving that they themselves had wrought the harm, thought that the Caraiman had sent sorrow upon them out of wanton cruelty and sport. They would no longer listen to the bagpipes, whose sweet strains had of old been wont to delight their ears. The old giant, indeed, did not often care to play on his pipes now. He had grown weary for very sorrow, and would sleep for hours together under the shade of his eyebrows, which had grown down into his beard. But sometimes he would start up out of sleep, put the pipes to his mouth, and blow a very trumpet-blast out into the wicked world. Hence there at last arose such a raging storm that the trees ground, creaking and groaning, against one another, and caused a fire to burst out, so that soon the whole forest was in flames. Then he reached up with the tree that grew upon his head, till he touched the clouds, and shook down rain to quench the fire.

But all this while the human beings below had only one thought—how to put the bagpipes to silence forever and ever. So they set out with lances and spears, and slings and stones, to give battle to the giant; but at the sight of them he burst into such laughter that an earthquake took place, which swallowed them all up, with their dwellings and their cattle. Then another host set out against him with pine-torches, wherewith to set his beard on fire. He did but sneeze, however, and all the torches were extinguished, and their bearers fell backward to the earth. A third host would have bound him while he slept, but he stretched his limbs, and the bonds burst, and all the men about him were crushed to atoms. Then they would have set upon him all the mighty wild beasts he had created; but he swept the air together and made thereof an endless fall of snow, that covered them over and over, and buried them deep, and turned to ice above them; so that, after thousands of years, when their like was no more to be seen on earth, those beasts still lay, with fur and flesh unchanged, embedded in the ice.

Then they bethought themselves of getting hold of the bagpipes by stealth and carrying them off while the giant was asleep. But he laid his head upon them, and it was so heavy that men and beasts together could not drag the pipes from under it. So at last they crept up quite softly and bored a tiny hole in the bagpipes — and lo! there arose such a storm that one could not tell earth or sea or sky apart, and scarcely anything survived of all that the Caraiman had created. But the giant awoke no more; he is still slumbering, and under his arm are the bagpipes, which sometimes begin to sound, when the storm-wind catches in them as it hurries down the Prahova valley. If only someone could but mend the bagpipes, then the world would belong to the children once more.

—From *Legends from River and Mountain* by Carmen Sylva (H.M. the Queen of Roumania) and Alma Strettell, 1896.

—❖—

Then the piper and couples advancing,
Pumps, brogues, and bare feet fell a-prancing;
Such piping, such figuring and dancing,
was ne'er known at Ballyporeen.
From the traditional song
"The Wedding of Ballyporeen"

Caoch the Piper

One winter's day, long, long, ago,
When I was a little fellow,
A piper wandered to our door,
Grey-headed, blind and yellow—
And, oh! how glad was my young heart,
Though earth and sky look'd dreary—
To see the stranger and his dog—
Poor "Pinch" and Caoch O'Leary.

And when he stowed away his "bag,"
Cross-barr'd with green and yellow,
I thought and said, "in Ireland's ground,
There's not so fine a fellow."
And Fineen Burke and Shane Magee,
And Eily, Kate, and Mary,
Rushed in, with panting haste to "see,"
And "welcome" Caoch O'Leary.

Oh! God be with those happy times,
Oh! God be with my childhood,
When I, bare-headed, roamed all day,
Bird-nesting in the wild-wood—
I'll not forget those sunny hours,
However years may vary;
I'll not forget my early friends,
Nor honest Caoch O'Leary.

Poor Caoch and "Pinch" slept well that night,
And in the morning early,
He called me up to hear him play
"The wind that shakes the barley."
And then he stroked my flaxen hair,
And cried—"God mark my deary,"

And how I wept when he said "farewell,
And think of Caoch O'Leary."

And seasons came and went, and still
Old Caoch was not forgotten,
Although I thought him "dead and gone,"
And in the cold clay rotten.
And often when I walked and danced,
With Eily, Kate, and Mary,
We spoke of childhood's rosy hours,
And prayed for Caoch O'Leary.

Well—twenty summers had gone past,
And June's red sun was sinking,
When I, a man, sat by my door,
Of twenty sad things thinking.
A little dog came up the way,
His gait was slow and weary,
And at his tail a lame man limped—
Twas "Pinch" and Caoch O'Leary!

Old Caoch! but ah! how woe-begone!
His form is bowed and bending,
His fleshless hands are stiff and wan,
Ay—Time is even blending
The colours on his thread-bare "bag"—
And "Pinch" is twice as hairy
And "thin-spare" as when first I saw
Himself and Caoch O'Leary.

"God's blessing here," the wanderer cried,
"Far, far, be hell's black viper;
Does anybody hereabouts,
Remember Caoch the Piper?"
With swelling heart I grasped his hand;
The old man murmured "deary!

Are you the silky-headed child,
That lov'd poor Caoch O'Leary?"

"Yes, yes," I said—the wanderer wept
As if his heart was breaking—
"And where, *a vhic machree*," he sobbed,
"Is all the merry-making,
I found here twenty years ago?"—
"My tale," I sighed, "might weary,
Enough to say—there's none but me,
To welcome Caoch O'Leary."

"Vo, Vo, Vo!" the old man cried,
And wrung his hands in sorrow.
"Pray lead me in, *asthore machree*,
And I'll go home to-morrow.
My 'peace is made'—I'll calmly leave
This world so cold and dreary,
And you shall keep my pipes and dog,
And pray for Caoch O'Leary."

With "Pinch," I watched his bed that night,
Next day, his wish was granted;
He died—and Father James was brought,
And the Requiem Mass was chanted—
The neighbours came;—we dug his grave,
Near Eily, Kate, and Mary,
And there he sleeps his last sweet sleep—
God rest you! Caoch O'Leary.

—From *Legends and Poems by John Keegan,*
edited by Rev. J. Canon O'Hanlon, 1907.

The Piper Came to Our Town

The Hundred Pipers

Wi' a hundred pipers[1], an' a', an' a',
Wi' a hundred pipers, an' a', an' a',
We'll up, and we'll gi'e them a blaw, a blaw,
Wi' a hundred pipers, an' a', an' a'.
It is ower the border, awa', awa',
It is ower the border, awa', awa',
Oh, we'll on, an' we'll march to Carlisle ha',
Wi' its yetts, its castel, an' a', an' a'.

Oh, our brave sodger lads look'd braw, an' braw,
Wi' their tartans, their kilts, an' a', an' a',
Wi' bannets an' feathers, an' glittrin' gear,
An' pibrochs soundin' sae sweet an' clear.
Will they a' come hame to their ain dear glen?
Will they a' return, our brave Hieland men?
Oh, second-sighted Sandie look'd fu' wae,
An' mithers grat sair whan they march'd away.
Wi' a hundred pipers, &c.

Oh, wha is the foremaist o' a', o' a' ?
Wha is it first follows the blaw, the blaw?
Bonnie Charlie, the king o' us a', us a',
Wi' his hundred pipers, an' a', an' a'.
His bannet and feather, he's waving high,
His prancin' steed maist seems to fly;
The nor' wind plays wi' his curly hair,
While the pipers blaw up an unco flare!
Wi' his hundred pipers, &c.

---

1. "Charles Edward entered Carlisle preceded by a hundred pipers. Two thousand Highlanders crossed the Esk, at Longtown; the tide being swollen, nothing was seen of them but their heads and shoulders; they stemmed the force of the stream, and lost not a man in the passage: when landed, the pipers struck up, and they danced reels until they were dry again." —From "Authentic Account of Occupation of Carlisle," by George G. Monsey, from *The Modern Scottish Minstrel*, 1855.

The Esk was swollen sae red an' sae deep,
But shouther to shouther the brave lads keep;
Twa thousand swam ower to fell English ground,
An' danced themselves dry to the pibroch sound.
Dumfounder'd the English were a', were a',
Dumfounder'd they a' heard the blaw, the blaw,
Dumfounder'd they a' ran awa', awa',
Frae the hundred pipers, an' a', an' a'.
Wi' a hundred pipers, &c.

—From *The Modern Scottish Minstrel, or The Songs of Scotland of
the Past Half Century* by Charles Rogers, 1855.

—❖—

*Yon squakin' saxophone gives me
the syncopated gripes.
I'm sick of jazz.
I want to hear the skirling of the pipes.*
Robert Service

Piper M'Nee

I winna sing sorrows, I ha'e nane to sing,
Nor mope owre the evils to-morrow may bring,
I'll tune up my reed on a happier key,
An' gi'e ye a lilt aboot Piper M'Nee.

The piper is windy an' weel he can blaw,
A' gloomy distempers he frichtens awa',
A cure mair effectual than whisky or tea,
Leaps forth frae the chanter o' Piper M'Nee.

He lives in a hoose by the side o' a burn,
Whaur the jucks an' the puddocks wallop in turn,
Tho' hairy and Hielan', an' fond o' a spree,
A capital piper is Piper M'Nee.

When the grey o' the gloamin' begins to come doon,
He screws up his pipes an' he pits them in tune.
Then laddies an' lassies o' every degree
Come loupin' an' laughin' roon' Piper M'Nee.

When Katie an' Lizzie come in frae the kye,
An' synd their milk coggies an' lay them a' by;
Then few are the gentry sae lichtsome as we,
Wha dance to the chanter o' Piper M'Nee.

Oor health is oor wealth, an' contentment oor store,
We always hae plenty, an' dainties galore;
We jump an' we thump, an' cry oot in oor glee,
"Success to the chanter o' Piper M'Nee."

Gran'faither is hoochin' an' crackin' his thooms,
An' granny's forgettin' her toothache an' rheums,
Their hearts are sae gladdened the young anes to see,
A' dance to the chanter o' Piper M'Nee.

The Piper Came to Our Town   173

The motties that trouble the too open eye,
They fash us but little, or never come nigh,
The dark spots o' the war!', if ony such be,
Are' scattered and brichtened by Piper M'Nee.

Oors are the pleasures that never breed pain,
That after-thochts sweeten an' seek for again,
Such pleasures as happy hearts ever shall pree,
That dance to the chanter o' Piper M'Nee.

If gout or rheumatics e'er trouble your banes,
Or the cares o' the warl' e'er jumble your brains,
Jist come to the Hielan's gin summer wi' me,
An' dance to the chanter o' Piper M'Nee.

If foemen should ever endeavour to land
Oor ticht little island, to brag or to brand,
The lads o' Balquhidder wad gie them their fee,
If led to the battle by Piper M'Nee.

Then health to the piper, an' blest be the feet
That trip it sae neatly to music sae sweet,
Lang may they be soople an' willin' an' free
To dance to the chanter o' Piper M'Nee.

> —by Finlay Farquharson, from *The Harp of Perthshire:*
> *A Collection of Songs, Ballads, and Other Poetical Pieces,*
> edited by Robert Ford, 1893.

The Piper o' Dundee

The piper came to our town, to our town, to our town,
The piper came to our town, and he play'd bonnilie.
He play'd a spring, the laird to please,
A spring brent new from 'yont the seas,
And then he gae his bags a wheeze
And play'd anither key.
And wasna he a roguy, a roguy, a roguy,
And wasna he a roguy, the piper o' Dundee?

He play'd "The Welcome ower the Main," And "Ye'se be fou
and I'se be fain," and "Auld Stuart's back again,"
Wi' muckle mirth and glee.
And wasna he a roguy, a roguy, a roguy,
And wasna he a roguy, the piper o' Dundee?

He play'd "The Kirk", he play'd "The Queer,"
    "The Mullin Dhu," and "Chevalier,"
And "Lang away, but welcome here,"
    Sae sweet, sae bonnilie.
And wasna he a roguy, a roguy, a roguy,
And wasna he a roguy, the piper o' Dundee?

It's some gat swords and some gat nane,
And some were dancing mad their lane,
And mony a vow o' weir was ta'en, that night at Amulrie.
And wasna he a roguy, a roguy, a roguy,
And wasna he a roguy, the piper o' Dundee?

There was Tullibardine and Burleigh
And Struan, Keith, and Olgivie,
And brave Carnegie, wha but he,
The piper o' Dundee?

—From *Jacobite Minstrelsy*, 1828.

Music for the Road

[The bagpipes seem] to have been considered a cheering adjunct to a long journey, and so Chaucer's pilgrims were brought out of town to the strains of the Miller's pipe. Early in the fifteenth century we find the following reason given:

> I say to thee that it is right well done that Pylgremys have with them both singers and also pipers, that when one of them that goeth barefoote, striketh his too upon a stone, and hurteth hym sore and maketh hym to blede, it is well done that he and his fellow begyn then a Songe, or else take out of his bosome a Baggepipe for to drive away with soche myrthe the hurte of his felow.

—Excerpt from *Old English Instruments of Music: Their History and Character* by Francis William Galpin, 1910.

—❖—

Bagpipes and the Clergy

[T]he clergy were permitted to play [the bagpipes] if they would or could, for in *Vernon's Hunting of Purgatory to Death*, issued in 1561, the following "true tale" is told:

> I knewe a Priest whiche, when any of his parishioners should be maryed, woulde take his Backe-pipe and go fetch them to the Churche, playnge sweetely afoure them, and then would he laye his Instrument handsomely upon the Aultare, tylle he had maryed them and sayd Masse. Which thyng being done, he would gentillye bringe them

home againe with Backe-pipe. Was not this Priest a true Ministrell, thynke ye? for he dyd not conterfayt the Ministrell, but was one in dede.

On the other hand, in the year 1592, at Skilgate, in Somersetshire, Humphrey Sydenham was summoned for interrupting divine service by "causing the bells to be rung, and dyvers baggepipes to be blown, to the grete dishonour of Almighty God."

—Excerpt from *Old English Instruments of Music: Their History and Character* by Francis William Galpin, 1910.

—❖—

The Pibroch's Notes

A nation mourning for a fallen King;
The tears of women over Flodden Field:
The doom of Scotland by a compact sealed;
A group of Highlanders who faithful cling
To their young Chevalier, and wildly sing
The clansmen's war songs, soon again to wield
The claymore at Culloden, ne'er to yield
While Cumberland has forces left to wring
The life blood from those Scots whom none can bind.
The pibroch's notes no more thro' mountain wind,
But far away in solitary glen,
List to the sob of broken-hearted men!
'Tis changed—now minstrelsy and dance enthrall.
All these the bagpipe's wild weird strains recall.

— From *A Score of Sonnets* by William Burt Harlow, 1906.
Originally titled "The Bagpipe."

Thoughts o' Langsyne

The bagpipe's wild music comes o'er the broad lea,
An' the thoughts o' langsyne it is bringing to me,
When the warrior's post on the heather was placed,
When his heart and his hand for the combat was braced,
When the free and the brave to the battle were led,
An' when ilka man's hand had to keep his ain head.
Then auld-warld fancies my heart winna tyne,
O' the bauld and the true o' the days o' langsyne.

When the bairn was born the bagpipes were brought;
The first sound in its ear was their bauld-speaking note:
And when forth came the tartan in battle array,
The proud voice o' war aye was leading the way;
And when dead wi' his fathers the warrior was laid,
Abune his low dwellin' the coronach was play'd,
In weal, as in wae—amid tears, amid wine,
The bagpipe aye moved the bauld hearts o' langsyne.

Alang the hill side comes the pibroch's sound
An' auld Scottish thoughts frae my heart are unwound;
The days o' the past are around me again—
The hall o' the chieftain—the field o' the slain—
The men o' the plaid and the bonnet sae blue,
Wha by Scotland, my country, stude leally and true;
O! the land o' the thistle and bagpipe is mine,
Wi' its auld rousin' thoughts o' the days o' langsyne!

—by Robert Nicoll, from *The British Minstrel* and *Musical and
Literary Miscellany,* 1843. Originally titled "The Bagpipes."

The Piper Came to Our Town

Maggie Lauder

Wha wadnae be in love
    Wi' bonnie Maggie Lauder!
A piper met her gaun to Fife,
    And spier'd what was't they ca'd her:
Right scornfully thus answered she,
    Begone, you hallan-shaker;
Jog on your gate, you blether-skate!
    My name is Maggie Lauder.

Maggie, quoth he, now by my bags,
    I'm fidging fain to see you,
Sit down by me, my bonnie bird,
    In troth I winna steer you;
For I'm a piper to my trade;
    My name is Rab the Ranter:
The lasses loup as they were daft,
    When I blaw up my chanter.

Piper, quo Meg, have you your bags,
    And is your drone in order?
If ye be Rab, I've heard o' you,—
    Live you upon the border?
The lasses a', baith far and near,
    Have heard o' Rab the Ranter—
I'll shake my foot wi' right good will,
    If ye'll blaw up your chanter.

Then to his bags he flew wi' speed,
    About the drone he twisted;
Meg up and wallope'd o'er the green,
    For brawlie could she frisk it!
Weel done, quoth he; play up! quoth she;
    Weel bobbed! quoth Rab the Ranter;

'Tis worth my while to play, indeed,
   When I get sic a dancer!

Weel hae ye played your part, quoth Meg;
   Your cheeks are like the crimson—
There's nane in Scotland plays sae weel,
   Sin' we lost Habbie Simpson.
I've lived in Fife, baith maid and wife,
   These ten years and a quarter;
Gin ye should come to Anster Fair,
   Spier ye for Maggie Lauder.

   —Francis Semple, from *Songs of Scotland, Ancient and Modern*
                                    by Allan Cunningham, 1825.

In the notes to the original, Cunningham writes: Much idle controversy has arisen respecting the meaning of this admirable song: certain sensitive critics imagine the story to be an impure allegory, like "The Fleming Barge," while others accept the strict and literal and honest meaning of the words. It was written by Francis Semple about the year 1650, if we may trust family tradition. Tradition has lately accepted the aid of some very suspicious anecdotes, accompanied by oral verses, confirmatory of the claim of Semple to this song, and it would be well if the family would set such matters at rest. Under the name of "Mogey Lauther" this song was a favourite in England at the Restoration.

— ❖ —

They hired a fiddler and piper
An' stuck them on top of a barrel,
With a jug full of whisky between 'em
To kep them from having a quarrel.
From the traditional song "Mrs. McLaughlin's Party"

The Fairy Piper

And seated on a sapphire throne I saw the Fairy Queen;
And all the Red Branch heroes clad in armor dazzling bright
Lined up around the fairy mound; it was a splendid sight!

Then suddenly an elfin door oped wide in Ross-na-Ree,
A spell of gladness held the earth, and swayed
      each flow'r and tree,
And out there trooped the Fairy Folk,
      ten thousand strong if one,
All dancing in the sunshine, round about their haunted dun!

The hours flew by like moments, and the
      daylight faded soon,
Yet still went on that wondrous dance
      beneath a mystic moon;
My eyes grew dim with happiness, but when I
      gazed once more,
The vision all had vanished and the fairy spell was o'er!

Yet often since, in gladsome dream, I hear that piper play,
And feel again the rapture of that blissful summer day,
And often, too, I wander by the Rath of Ross-na-Ree,
Though now I know its magic door will ope no more to me!

—From *Irish Lyrics and Ballads* by Rev. James B. Dollard, 1917.

The Kintalen Changeling

There was living in Kintalen a woman who had a male-child with neither growth nor the bloom of other children of his age. From morning to evening he would not cease one minute from crying, and he would eat far more food than was natural for the like of him.

It was Harvest, and there was not a person on the farm who could draw a sickle but was out on the reaping field, except the mother of the child. She, too, would have been out were it not for fear that the nasty screaming thing would break his heart crying, if she should leave him in charge of any other person.

It happened that there was at the time a tailor in the house, making clothes. The tailor was a shrewd, observant man, and he was but a short time within until he became suspicious of the lad in the cradle. "You," he said to the woman, "may go to the reaping, and I will take care of the child."

The woman went away. But she had barely taken her feet over the threshold when the withered object she had left behind began shrieking and crying loudly and sorely. The tailor listened to him a good while, keeping his eye on him, till he was sure that he was nothing but a changeling. He now lost patience with him, and cried in a sharp, angry voice, "Stop that music, lad, or I'll put thee on the fire." The crying ceased for awhile, but afterwards it began a second time. "Art thou at it again, piper of the one tune?" said the tailor. "Let me hear that music anymore from thee, and I will kill thee with my dirk." When the faerie beheld the frown on the tailor's countenance and the dirk in his hand, he took such a fright that he kept quiet a good while. The tailor was a cheerful man, and to keep from wearying he began to hum a tune. In the middle of the music the ugly elf raised a loud howl. But, if he did, he was not allowed to go on with his warble but a very short time. The tailor leaped off his work-table, went, dirk in one hand and his sack in the other, to the cradle and said to the faerie, "We have had enough of that music; take these right great bagpipes and give us a tune on them, or else I'll put the dirk in thee." The faerie sat up in the cradle, took the pipes, and struck up the sweetest music the tailor had ever heard. The reapers heard it on the field, and instantly dropped their sickles and stood listening to the faerie music. At length they left the field, and ran in the direction whence the music came. But before they reached the house the tune had ceased; and they knew not who played it or whence it came.

When the reapers returned home in the evening, and the tailor got the mistress of the house alone, he told her everything that happened while she was at the reaping, and that her child was nothing but a changeling. He then told her to go with him to the Ardsheal side of the bay, and to throw him out in the loch. She did as was told her, and as soon as the nasty little elf touched the water he became a big grey-haired old man, and swam to the other side of the bay. When he got his feet on dry land, he cried to her that if he had known beforehand what she was going to do he would have made her never think of doing such a thing again.

She returned home and found her own child at the door before her, hale and sound, and without memory of what had happened.

—Adapted from *Folk Tales and Fairy Lore in Gaelic and English*
by James MacDougall, 1910.

—❖—

Come, piper, play the "Shaskan Reel,"
Or else the "Lasses on the Heather,"
And Mary, lay aside your wheel
Until we dance once more together.
From the traditional song "Donal Kenny"

The Pipes at Lucknow

Lucknow is the capital city of Uttar Pradesh, today the most populous state of India. The Siege of Lucknow was the prolonged defence of the Residency during the Indian Rebellion of 1857 (also known as the First War of Indian Independence). After two successive relief attempts had reached the city, the defenders and civilians were evacuated from the Residency, which was abandoned.

PIPES of the misty moorlands,
    Voice of the glens and hills;
The droning of the torrents,
    The treble of the rills!
Not the braes of broom and heather,
    Nor the mountains dark with rain,
Nor maiden bower, nor border tower,
    Have heard your sweetest strain!

Dear to the Lowland reaper,
    And plaided mountaineer,—
To the cottage and the castle
    The Scottish pipes are dear;—
Sweet sounds the ancient pibroch
    O'er mountain, loch, and glade;
But the sweetest of all music
    The Pipes at Lucknow played.

Day by day the Indian tiger
    Louder yelled, and nearer crept;
Round and round the jungle-serpent
    Near and nearer circles swept.
"Pray for rescue, wives and mothers,—
    Pray to-day!" the soldier said;
"To-morrow, death's between us
    And the wrong and shame we dread."

The Piper Came to Our Town

Oh, they listened, looked, and waited,
    Till their hope became despair;
And the sobs of low bewailing
    Filled the pauses of their prayer.
Then up spake a Scottish maiden,
    With her ear unto the ground:
"Dinna ye hear it?—dinna ye hear it?
    The pipes o' Havelock sound!"

Hushed the wounded man his groaning;
    Hushed the wife her little ones;
Alone they heard the drum-roll
    And the roar of Sepoy guns.
But to sounds of home and childhood
    The Highland ear was true;—
As her mother's cradle-crooning
    The mountain pipes she knew.

Like the march of soundless music
    Through the vision of the seer,
More of feeling than of hearing,
    Of the heart than of the ear,
She knew the droning pibroch,
    She knew the Campbell's call:
"Hark! hear ye no' MacGregor's,—
    The grandest o' them all!"

Oh, they listened, dumb and breathless,
    And they caught the sound at last;
Faint and far beyond the Goomtee
    Rose and fell the piper's blast!
Then a burst of wild thanksgiving
    Mingled woman's voice and man's;
"God be praised!—the march of Havelock!
    The piping of the clans!"

Louder, nearer, fierce as vengeance,
    Sharp and shrill as swords at strife,
Came the wild MacGregor's clan-call,
    Stinging all the air to life.
But when the far-off dust-cloud
    To plaided legions grew,
Full tenderly and blithesomely
    The pipes of rescue blew!

Round the silver domes of Lucknow,
    Moslem mosque and Pagan shrine,
Breathed the air to Britons dearest,
    The air of Auld Lang Syne.
O'er the cruel roll of war-drums
    Rose that sweet and homelike strain;
And the tartan clove the turban,
    As the Goomtee cleaves the plain.

Dear to the corn-land reaper
    And plaided mountaineer,—
To the cottage and the castle
    The piper's song is dear.
Sweet sounds the Gaelic pibroch
    O'er mountain, glen, and glade;
But the sweetest of all music
    The Pipes at Lucknow played!

—by John Greenleaf Whittier, from *Poetical Works of John Greenleaf Whittier,* 1888.

The Piper Came to Our Town

The Relief of Lucknow

September 26, 1857.

Oh, that last day in Lucknow fort!
    We knew that it was the last;
That the enemy's lines crept surely on,
    And the end was coming fast.

To yield to that foe meant worse than death;
    And the men and we all worked on;
It was one day more of smoke and roar,
    And then it would all be done.

There was one of us, a corporal's wife,
    A fair, young, gentle thing,
Wasted with fever in the siege,
    And her mind was wandering.

She lay on the ground, in her Scottish plaid,
    And I took her head on my knee;
"When my father comes hame frae the pleugh," she said,
    "Oh! then please wauken me."

She slept like a child on her father's floor,
    In the flecking of woodbine-shade,
When the house-dog sprawls by the open door,
    And the mother's wheel is stayed.

It was smoke and roar and powder-stench,
    And hopeless waiting for death;
And the soldier's wife, like a full-tired child,
    Seemed scarce to draw her breath.

I sank to sleep; and I had my dream

Of an English village-lane,
And wall and garden;—but one wild scream
    Brought me back to the roar again.

There Jessie Brown stood listening
    Till a sudden gladness broke
All over her face; and she caught my hand
    And drew me near as she spoke:—

"The Hielanders! O! dinna ye hear
    The slogan far awa'?
The McGregor's. O! I ken it weel;
    It's the grandest o' them a'!

"God bless the bonny Hielanders!
    We're saved! we're saved!" she cried;
And fell on her knees; and thanks to God
    Flowed forth like a full flood-tide.

Along the battery-line her cry
    Had fallen among the men,
And they started back;—they were there to die;
    But was life so near them, then?

They listened for life; the rattling fire
    Far off, and the far-off roar,
Were all; and the colonel shook his head,
    And they turned to their guns once more.

But Jessie said, "The slogan's done;
    But winna ye hear it noo,—
The Campbells are comin'? It's no a dream;
    Our succors hae broken through!"

We heard the roar and the rattle afar,
    But the pipes we could not hear;

So the men plied their work of hopeless war,
    And knew that the end was near.

It was not long ere it made its way,—
    A thrilling, ceaseless sound:
It was no noise from the strife afar,
    Or the sappers under ground.

It *was* the pipes of the Highlanders!
    And now they played *Auld Lang Syne*,
It came to our men like the voice of God,
    And they shouted along the line.

And they wept, and shook one another's hands,
    And the women sobbed in a crowd;
And every one knelt down where he stood,
    And we all thanked God aloud.

That happy time, when we welcomed them,
    Our men put Jessie first;
And the general gave her his hand, and cheers
    Like a storm from the soldiers burst.

And the pipers' ribbons and tartans streamed,
    Marching round and round our line;
And our joyful cheers were broken with tears,
    As the pipes played *Auld Lang Syne*.

—by Robert Traill Spence Lowell, from *The Home Book of Verse:*
    American and English 1580–1912, selected and arranged
                    by Burton Egbert Stevenson, 1915.

The Piper Came to Our Town   189

The Piper and the Changeable Fairy

Versified from T. Crofton Croker

Of all the strange doings and all the vagaries
Recounted at length about goblins and fairies,
There is nothing the fairy-lore student surprises
So much as their many and varied disguises.
The one I shall tell of had changes as many
As the great Mister Woodin, and he could beat any
That I ever read of who wasn't a fairy;
'Twas he who once frightened half fair Tipperary.
But first I must tell you there lived in that county
    Larry Hoolan, a piper, a very great player,
Who lived by his piping, that is, on the bounty
Of those that he played to at wedding or fair.

In old times the fairies selected odd places
Which they kept to themselves: they were called "fairy ground;"
The farmers all knew them because of the traces
They left where they'd dauced in their circles around.

And these, in old times, they devoutly respected,
Because they believed that the fairies protected
Their crops from the vermin, their cows from the cramp,
Their pigs from the measles, their malt from the damp,
And goodness knows what! So the fairies and elves
Were left on each farm a snug spot to themselves.

Now, a farmer, it chanced, had some fairy-ground taken,
Which the elves for a season had held, then forsaken,
And when they came back there, for peace and for quiet,
His bulls and his cows all kicked up such a riot,

The fairies not only could get no repose,
But they couldn't go dancing whenever they chose;
And so they resolved that they would, come what may,
The farmer and all his men frighten away.

The herdsman he slept in the fields all the night,
And him they resolved they would first put to flight.
Their chief he came down from their home on the hill,
When the moon it shone bright and the winds they were still,
The herdsman he pinched, just to keep him awake,
And the very first form he determined to take
Was a little lame man with the head of a bull,
And a tail—which he asked the poor herdsman to pull.
The herdsman objected—the fairy became
A dragon, with eyes like a forge in a flame,
And the herdsman he asked if he'd into them blow?
And the herdsman replied, very nervously, "No."
And then he changed into a horse with huge wings,
And asked him to ride and "lay hold of them things;"
And then, as the poor herdsman tried to escape,
He suddenly changed to a great hairy ape,
With the feet of a duck and a turkey-cock's tail,
And he asked him if he'd through the air take a sail?
And so he went on till the daylight appeared,
When he changed, yet again, to a cow with a beard,
And galloped away round the foot of the hill,
And left the poor herdsman, half dead, quaking still.
The herdsman he went from the farmer outright,
For nought could induce him to stay the next night;
So he hired another, and he did the same—
Another!—all left him as soon as they came!
Their wages he rose, but the thing never mended,
And at last the poor bulls and cows went unattended;
And these, too, the fairies would not let alone,
But worried them till they were all skin and bone,
So determined were they that not one should be found

Alive to molest them on their fairy-ground.

The farmer well knew that his rent he must pay,
And yet all his substance was melting away;
His beasts at the market no money would make,
They'd laugh at him there should he venture to take
Such scarecrows! So what was—what was to be done?
To ruin he must go, and that with a run!

At last Larry Hoolan came into his head;
The piper feared nothing—at least so 'twas said;
Give him plenty of whisky he'd fight a whole fair,
Tho' that's but Dutch courage some people declare.
However, 'tis certain that Larry was bold
And brave as a lion, just as he'd been told:
So when he was sent for to come to the farm,
And the farmer had told him his fear and alarm,
"If that's all the matter," said Larry, "I'll come—
I was never afraid of a hop o' my thumb—
And as to their shapes, let them take what they will,
I'll watch for a week at the foot of the hill;
And if that I fail all the time there to tarry,
Say, you're not the farmer, and my name's not Larry!"
The farmer replied, "Larry, don't be too bold,
Take this bottle of whisky to keep out the cold;
And if you indeed get the best of the strife
You're free of my dish and my cellar for life."
And so 'twixt the two men the bargain was struck,
And the farmer wished Larry "good night and good luck."

Now Larry he thought that, to keep him awake,
To the foot of the hill he his bagpipes would take:
So he made himself snug, and sat down on a stone,
And the wind-bag he pressed with a squeak and a drone.
But he hadn't played long when the fairies came out
To see what the squalls and the grunts were about.

"Another man here at the foot of the hill!
Does that wretched old farmer defy us, then, still?"
Exclaimed, as he spied out the piper, a fairy—
But all Larry did was to play "Paddy Carey."
And then the same one that the herdsman had frightened
Came up to the piper—and, as the moon brightened,
Betwixt it and Larry, without any pause,
There he stood, a great cat, on the tips of his claws,—
A cat twice as large as the largest black Bruin—
That began, with the voice of a water-mill, mewing:
"Hurroo!" cried the piper, "I'm up to your gammon!"
Then it turned itself round and jumped up as a salmon,
A salmon that danced the grass, heather, and roots on,
With a yellow cravat and a pair of top-boots on!
"Hurroo!" cried the piper again, blithe and gay,
"Go it, jewel, as long as you dance I can play."
So he struck up a lilt, and he played it so rarely
That the dance knocked the funny fish out of breath fairly.
At this Larry Hoolan did nothing but laugh,
So the fairy he instantly changed to a calf,
And Larry, who courage was ne'er known to lack,
Cried "Hurroo!" once again, and jumped up on his back
The fairy now thought that he fairly had caught him;
But Larry rode well, for a horse jockey taught him,
And when the calf galloped him off to the hill
And got to the top, he was sitting there still.

The height of this hill, just to give you a notion,
Was so great you could see the broad Atlantic ocean,
And just at its base was fair Limerick City,
With its women so lovely, its men all so witty;
Its ships and its docks, and its quays and its bridges,
And the fields all around with their furrows and ridges;
And there too was seen, that clear bright rippling river,
So famous in song, that goes singing for ever;
Though never till then had the broad flowing Shannon

Been leaped, at a jump, by a calf with a man on ;
But then it was done—for the fairy leaped over
And landed the piper in a field of red clover.
'Twas done in a second, though ten miles or more,
Was the hill that they'd left on the opposite shore:
And Larry exclaimed, with "Hurroo!" and a laugh,
"By St. Patrick! that's not a bad leap—*for a calf.*"

The fairy, astounded, then changed to himself,
For though he was ever a mischievous elf,
He still was an elf who was open to reason,
And he loved a good joke when 'twas not out of season;
So he said to the piper, "Such courage you've shown,
That with one trial more I will leave you alone;—
Should you like to go back ?" "If to you all the same,"
Said the piper, "I'd like to go back as I came."
"Agreed!" said the fairy, then changed to the calf,
And the piper again he jumped up with a laugh,
And again they went up like a bounding balloon,
And, the piper declares, very near touched the moon,
For it took them three minutes before they came down
At the foot of the hill near fair Limerick town.

The fairy then bade Larry Hoolan good night,
And told him next day they'd be rid of them quite;
That they'd a new fairy-ground look for elsewhere,
And the lands of the farmer in future would spare.
The piper he went to the farmer in glee,
And he lived at the farm, and contented was he;
He married his daughter, who made a good wife,
And found himself very well "tiled-in" for life;
And the hill, as you'll find if you pass by that way,
Is " the hill of the Fairy Calf" called to this day.

—From *Penny Readings in Prose and Verse*,
selected and edited by J. E. Carpenter, 1866

The Piper Came to Our Town

To the Lion Rampant

Did you hear the light feet marching,
Marching down the birchclad glen?
Did ye see the pipers' streamers,
Floating free behind the men?
Did ye hear the brave tunes ringing,
As they swung the drones on high?
Did ye watch the rhythm of the kilt,
Did ye hear the war march die?
Behind the sharp bend of the road,
Beyond the wild Ben Nevis range:
The strains of Donald Dubh again,
Bore out the clans to battles strange.
But, it's o! our tears ran sorely,
As they left the Scottish shore;
For who'd come back, and who would see
Lochaber's wooded braes no more?
Only the Lord of Hosts could tell,
And the wae heart's own prophetic knell.

Did ye see the brave lads smiling,
As they drew their bonnets down,
With the shortened breath indrawn and tight,
The flashing eyes, the steadfast frown?
Did ye hear the whistling shot and shell,
That swept the kilted foremost ranks
Like the snow wind's call before its fall,
As clouds lie piled in fleecy banks?
Ah, no! 'Twas not the keen gust bite,
That reddens cheeks with healthful glow,
Nor the hissing as the shrapnel fell
The sound of melting, driving snow.
Did ye hear the war pipes calling,
Like the mavis, in the van,

'Mid the thunder of the battle storm,
To the valour of each Scottish man?
The blood call of the march they knew,
With bayonet charge was answered true.
O! Piper lads! O! Piper lads!
What magic woven spell
Amergin breathed within your reeds,
Is not for mortal voice to tell.
The wizard winds thro' reed and drone,
The soul draws on to follow after
To splendid heights of hero and fame,
Or, spellbound, led to grim disaster.
Great Fingal heard beyond the hills
Your quivering grace notes heavenward soar;
Old Ossian followed in a dream
The "Broom of Peril" Oscar bore.
Blow softly, then, O! Piobaireachd's wail,
Or loud and bold, to stir the heart;
No music stirs as yours can stir,
Wild glamour of the Fairies' Art.

Did ye hear the war pipes shrilling,
Out beyond the German lines,
Where the gallant soldiers pressing on,
Drove home their charge, despite the mines?
Did ye see yon brave lad casting
His broken pipes aside,
As he plunged among the German lines
To do his part what'er betide?
Did ye watch the tartans puring down
From hill, and trench, and sweep
The cruel Teuton from the field,
Like herds of driven sheep?
Did ye hear the shot that echoed,
Till it reached a woodland lone?
Did ye see the mother's auld grey plaid,

The Piper Came to Our Town

Wrapped round her mourning head? —Ochone!
Did ye see the tears that dropped like rain,
For the lads we ne'er may see again?

O! Piper lads! O! Piper lads!
What magic woven spell
Amergin breathed within your reeds,
Is not for mortal voice to tell.
The wizard winds thro' reed and drone,
The soul draws on to follow after
To splendid heights of hero and fame,
Or, spellbound, led to grim disaster.
Great Fingal heard beyond the hills
Your quivering grace notes heavenward soar;
Old Ossian followed in a dream
The "Broom of Peril" Oscar bore.
Blow softly, then, O! Piobaireachd's wail,
Or loud and hold, to stir the heart;
No music stirs as yours can stir,
Wild glamour of the Fairies' Art.

True hearts, as ever ready,
to guard their native land,
O! Scotland's sons are bonnie,
and Scotland's sons are grand.
True hearts that never failed her yet,
today as yester year. O! Scotia rouse thine echoes,
with one resounding cheer.
Let the Lion Rampant proudly raise
his head on cloth of gold,
For the deeds of valour done today,
in pages yet untold.
Gay Gordon lads, brave Seaforths,
Black Watch and Camerons tell,
What steeled your dauntless hearts to face that living screen of hell!
The pipes of Loos, of Mons, of far and distant Dardanelles,

That spake in Gaelic tones to each
who dared those deadly shells.
The old time slogan of the race,
the spell that cannot fail,
"A chlanna nan gaidheal!
A chlanna nan, Gailheal!
Guillain ri Guillain a cheile!"

—by Alice C. MacDonell of Keppoch, from *The Pipes of War:*
A Record of the Achievements of Pipers of Scottish and Overseas
Regiments During the War, 1914-1918, by Bruce Gordon Seton,
John Grant, Neil Munro, Boyd Cable, and Philip Gibbs, 1920.

—❖—

Molleen oge, my Molleen oge,
Go put on your natest brogue,
And slip into your smartest gown,
You rosy little rogue;
For a message kind I bear
To yourself from ould Adair,
that Pat the piper's come around,
And there'll be dancin' there.
From the traditional song "Molleen Oge"

The Pipes: Onset

Dedicated to Major Angus MacGillivary

The cry is in my ear,
The sight is in my eye,
This is the dawning of the day
That shall see me die.

What is the piper playing
That battles in my blood?—
Winds in it,
Waves in it,
Waters at the flood;
Sadness in it,
Madness in it,
Weeping mists and rain—
What is the piper playing
That beats within my brain?

Sobbing and throbbing
Like a soul's unrest;
I drink his madd'ning music in
As milk at my mother's breast.
Flame in it,
Fame in it,
Love and desire;
The clean hills,
The clear rills,
The smouldering peat fire;
Glances sweet,
Dancing feet,
Beating on the floor,
Maidens fair,
Comrades rare

I shall meet no more.
The cry is in my ear,
The sight is in my eye,
This is the morning of the day,
That shall see me die.

What is the piper playing
That surges in my blood?
The soft breeze
In pine trees,
The hawthorn i' the bud.
The lone tarn,
The golden barn,
Fields of waving grain—
What is the piper playing
That beats within my brain?

Red war screams from his reeds
And in the thrumming drones
There lurks the lapping of men's blood,
And sobs, and dying groans.
Night in it,
Fight in it,
Wraiths of stricken men,
Ghosts of ancient clansmen
Sweeping down the glen.
Life in it,
Strife in it,
Whisp'rings—it is well,
If you bear a foemen down
Right to reddest hell!

What is the piper playing?
For now I may not hear...
The glamour comes across my soul,
and the cry is in my ear.

The Piper Came to Our Town

—by Lt. Joseph Lee, from *The Pipes of War: A Record of the Achievements of Pipers of Scottish and Overseas Regiments During the War, 1914–1918,* by Bruce Gordon Seton, John Grant, Neil Munro, Boyd Cable, and Philip Gibbs, 1920.

— ❖ —

Oh! The days of the Kerry dancing, oh!
The ring of the piper's tune.
Oh! For one of those hours of gladness, gone, alas!
Like youth, too soon.
When the boys began to gather
in the glen of a summer night,
and the Kerry piper's tuning
made us long with wild delight...
From the traditional song "Kerry Dance"

The Hereditary Pipers

The "people of peace" have ever been held to be gifted with music. When their green hillocks are open, music and song may be heard so sweet and alluring that the incautious mortal, unable to resist their charm, goes into the bower to join in the merriment and remains a half willing if sometimes unwitting prisoner, till some accident or a friend releases him. Then he finds that he has been a year and a day, seven, nine, or even twenty years in the fairy knoll, while he thought 'twas but an hour or a night, so beguiling were the music and the dance and the little folks themselves!

Many instruments the fairies have too—pipes and harps and other wind and stringed instruments, and all so greatly superior to those of human make that a fairy instrument is a coveted treasure among the people of earth. But not many of these have been bestowed on the children of men, and the few seem all to have been given by the women of faery. Here are some stories of fairy pipes which I have heard in the Hebrides, and now translate from Gaelic.

The famous Maccrimmons, pipers to the Macleods of Macleod, owed their renown in music to a fairy. When the Macleod of the day returned from one of the Crusades, he brought with him from Cremona a servant who, quite according to Highland usage, became known by the name of his home. Cremon married in Skye, and when his son was old enough he sent him to the school or college of music at Boreraig, in Glendale, to learn pipe music. This school was celebrated throughout Alban and Erin and Sasunn and the divisions of Europe, and had many pupils, especially for the bagpipes. Cremon wished his son to be a good piper, that he might obtain the honourable position of piper to Macleod of Macleod, for musicians were highly esteemed among the ancient Gaels, and the office of musician to a great chief was one of much honour and dignity,

The Piper Came to Our Town

conferring on its holder many valued privileges and possessions.

But "Mac Cremmain," or MacCrimmon, as he was called—the son of Cremon—had no aptitude for the Highland pipes; they were foreign to his race and nature, and his fellow-pupils held rather aloof from the strange lad whose ways were more of his father's land than of his mother's. So the lad was sorrowful and miserable, and he often went out with his sorrow and his misery to the lee of a green knoll at a little distance from the college, to brood and to wish that he could play the pipes like his fellow-students.

One day the "Piobaire mor"—great Piper, as the head of the college was called—got an invitation to the marriage of a great Chief, and he was asked to bring some of his pupils to help to entertain the guests. There was much excitement in the college, and much speculating and rivalry among the lads as to who would be thought worthy to go. When the Piobaire mor announced his choice of pupils, MacCrimmon's name was not among them, and though he had not really expected to be among those chosen, he was heavy and sad with disappointment. After the others had set out for the Chief's dun, MacCrimmon could no longer restrain his feelings, and he threw himself down in his lonely haunt on the green hillock and wept the tears—the bitter tears—of disappointed hope.

While he was dead to all around, he was startled by the sound of a voice asking why he grieved so greatly. Looking up he saw a woman, small indeed, but of beautiful face and form, dressed in a soft green gown, gazing at him with pity shining in her eyes, and peace and love in her face. He knew she was one of the "sithe" or fairies, and he was afraid. But she looked at him so tenderly and spoke to him so kindly that he poured out before her all his heart's heavy sorrow. He told her that he could not master the bagpipes, and that he played so badly that he had not been taken to the wedding, that the other pupils were not friendly, and that he was altogether miserable. The kind little fairy put her slender hand on the lad's dark head and comforted him, and she told him he would play better than any of the other students some day. She then gave him a chanter, the like of which had never been seen before by mortal eyes. She told him that the possessor of that chanter would carry with him "Buaidh na Piobaireachd"—the championship of piping. But should a word ever be said in disparagement of the chanter she would instantly take it back, with all the skill it conferred. Then the lovely green-robed fairy disappeared as mysteriously as she had come, leaving the lad too much lost in surprise to think of thanking her.

MacCrimmon hurried back to the college, put the chanter in the pipes and blew it. To his delight he found he could play, and not merely the tunes he had tried so unsuccessfully to learn but tunes he had never tried before, and even new tunes that no one had ever heard; and he could play them, too, better than any one he had ever listened to—better than the Piobaire mor himself! His happiness was now as great as his grief had been before, and he could hardly sleep or eat, he only wished to play his wonderful chanter night and day.

When his teacher and fellow-pupils returned after a few weeks' absence—for the festivities connected with the marriage of a great Chief were somewhat prolonged—they could scarcely believe their eyes and ears. The stupid foreign lad who could not play when they left, could now play better than the great Piper of the famous college of Boreraig! Quick questions were asked and the lad told his tale. All knew of the music of the "sithean" or fairy bower, and all knew that he to whom a "sithe" gave the gift of music was indeed endowed beyond all hope of rivalry. The wonderful chanter was examined and commented upon, but no one could make out of what material it was made. It did not seem to be made of metal, of wood, or of stone.

Those who had formerly jeered at MacCrimmon now envied him and vainly tried to imitate his playing. But it was useless. MacCrimmon could make his pipe move the hearts of his hearers so that they had no will but as it impelled them. Did he play "Geantraighe" they danced and sang for joy and pure happiness of mind and body. Did he play "Suaintraighe" they slumbered peacefully and with a happy smile dreamt of their dear ones and of pleasant days with their comrades. Did he play "Gultraighe" a wild pas-

The Piper Came to Our Town

sionate longing and a great sorrowful lamenting came into every heart. Never was such music heard before. From far and near people came to hear it and to wonder at it, and MacCrimmon's music played with their souls as the north wind plays with the leaves of the birch tree on the brown mountain side.

MacCrimmon became piper to Macleod of Macleod, and his son, and his son's sons succeeded him for many generations, and the fairy chanter descended as the most valued possession of the family. Their fame was known wherever music was loved. The college at Boreraig, where the first Maccrimmon had been so backward a learner, was under their teaching, and people came from Erin and from Sasunn and from all the divisions of Europe to learn music in Skye.

Before students were considered fit to leave the college—and the several courses lasted from four to ten years—they had to be able to play one hundred and ninety-nine tunes, some of them very intricate, besides exercises, and to be masters of theory and composition. It is said that in later days the Maccrimmons gave diplomas to successful graduates. These diplomas had on them pictures of Dunvegan Castle, of the galley of Macleod, and of various musical instruments, a seal, and the name of the holder, with the dates of entrance to and departure from the college. Two of the Macintyres of South Uist, hereditary musicians to Clanranald, were among the last students at this school—about the beginning of "the '45." Four cows are said to have been paid for their education there.

A Skye tradition says that it was practically the last of the Maccrimmon pipers who composed the beautiful and pathetic "cumha," or lament, known by his name, and that it has a double prophetic meaning in that it was a lament for himself, for he foresaw that he would be one of the many to give up life in the ill-fortuned Stuart wars, and also for the fairy's gift. This Maccrimmon was the only man killed at the Moy Rout, and after his death his son inherited the chanter and the office.

On one occasion Macleod of Dunvegan and Macleod of Raasay were returning in the Dunvegan galley after visiting the chief of

Abercrossain, now Applecross. Maccrimmon, as usual, was with his master and was asked to "seid suas"—blow up. He sat on the prow, the piper's seat, and began playing. But the wind was so strong and the sea so rough in the sound, that his fingers kept slipping off the chanter with the rolling of the galley. At last it got so bad that MacCrimmon threw down his pipes in anger, and began abusing the chanter because he could not keep his fingers on it. While he was speaking the chanter gave a leap over the side of the vessel into the sea. MacCrimmon remembered, too late, the command handed down by his fathers, for the chanter had gone as the fairy giver had said, so many generations before, that it would. And with the chanter went the championship of piping; and the home of the Maccrimmons is desolate, and their hereditary office unfilled. The set of pipes, called "an oiseach" with which the fairy chanter was used, is carefully kept at Dunvegan. Will the green-robed lady ever relent and return the chanter, and with it the championship of piping? Though indeed there are now no Maccrimmons in Skye to hold them.

Another legend is somewhat different. There was on a time a great gathering of pipers to be at Dunvegan, and there was no piper better than another far or near, on mainland or island, who did not take the road for the Dun. When the day came, there surely was the multitude of people—Macleods and strangers. It happened that Macleod of Dunvegan had a herd boy who was very wild to see the heros of the drones and to hear them for himself, and he asked Macleod if he might stay at home that day. "Thou little rascal that thou art," said Macleod, "thy work is tending the cattle; and good as piping is, it cannot keep the bulls from fighting, nor the calves from falling into the ditches. Away, boy, and do not return here till the black herdsman night brings thyself and the cattle home together." The lad went away downcast and disappointed, and drove the cattle to the shieling. He sat down on a fairy knoll and put the black chanter of the pipes in his mouth. But he had a scarf round his neck and his emotion was so great that his breath came in sudden jumps and leaps, and the chanter was but a bad stepmother to the pipes. At last he threw it away and hid

The Piper Came to Our Town

his head in a heather tuft for fear the dogs and the calves would see and mock at him. He had hardly put his head down when the "sithean" opened and the pretty little lady of melody came out. She put her white hand on the boy's head. "Bonnie lad," she said, "what has put against thee, and what harm has the black chanter of the pipe done thee?" He told her everything as it was, and how he himself wished things were. The lovely fairy then gave him his choice of three championships—the championship of sailing, so that his boat of spotted yew would cut a slender oaten straw, so good her steering, and that her keel would scrape as with sharp knives the limpets from the tops of the hidden rocks; or the championship of battle, so that the raven of the Dun would be satiated with the blood of his enemies every day on which the sun rose or darkness lay; or the championship of piping, so that he would bring the birds from the trees and that he would give peace and relief to wounded men and pain-worn women. The boy did not doubt nor delay in deciding which was better, the championships of sailing or of fighting, but without a word backward or forward he chose the championship of piping. Then the beautiful little fairy said, "Thou hast thy wish from this time," and she went back into the bower, and the knoll was as it had been before.

The boy stared at the place where she had been, but there was nothing to see—only soft green grass and flowers. He took up his pipes and played. But there was the wonderful thing! The music that was there! He had never known that there could be such music. And as he played the cattle and the dogs, and the deer of the hill, and the birds of the air, and the creeping things of the earth came round him to listen. After he had played for a long time he thought he would go away back to Dunvegan, for he felt he must tell everybody about the wonderful fairy and show them the gift she had given him. It was there the great piping was, on the green sward, and the many pipers from all places, and it was there the people were, gentle and simple in their crowds listening to them.

When Macleod saw the herd lad with his pipes under his arm listening with the others he was angry, and he asked him why he had left the cattle and come to the castle when he had given him fast orders to stay at the shieling. The lad answered that he could not keep away from the piping any longer, and that he felt sure he could play as well as the best piper there. Macleod laughed at the boy's presumption, but to punish him, told him to blow up, adding that if he failed to make good his boast he would get a hard thrashing. The boy blew up, and he played, and *that* was the playing and *that* was the music! At first the other pipers laughed, then they stared, then a great silence fell over them. When he had finished they all admitted that the herd lad had indeed "buaidh na piobaireachd," the championship of piping, and they eagerly crowded round him with questions. He told his tale, and then all said that he to whom the fairy queen of melody gave her gifts was indeed a musician, and they piped no more that day, for they said, "This young lad shames us all." The lad was taken from herding the cattle and made piper to Macleod of Dunvegan, and a good farm with its share of cattle and horses and sheep and goats was given to him and to his heirs so long as they should continue pipers to Dunvegan and follow its chief in war and in peace.

The hereditary musicians to the Macdonalds of Clanranald were Macintyres, and they too, got a gift of music from a fairy. This is how it was. A son of the musician—for the Macintyres were musicians before they got the fairy gift—had a sweetheart of the little people. She was a very beautiful lady with a skin like the fair breast of the kittiwake and cheeks like the wild red rose by the mountain stream. Her eyes were of the deep blue of the juniper-berry, and her long hair was the colour of soft, pale, un-wrought gold, that glimmered in the sun and fell about her like golden mist. Her voice was like sweet mellow music. The gown she had was of soft trailing stuff of the pure colour of the green sea when it lies over white sand, and as she walked it was like the moving light on a sloping field of long, green grass when the low wind blows over it and the sun's brightness is gently veiled. "Her steps were the music of song," and her fingers were so deft and quick that she could prepare a fleece of wool, pick it, and card it, and spin it, and dye it, and weave it into a big tartan plaid all in an hour by the sun; and her head and mind were so clever that she

The Piper Came to Our Town

knew even what was happening far off.

One evening when the fairy and young Macintyre were walking on the green flowery machair near to the farm of Smearclaid in South Uist that his father held as Clanranald's musician, she told him that strangers from Erin over the sea were coming to his father's house to hear if the Macintyres were indeed as good musicians as was reported. "But," the fairy said, "I will give you this reed, and you must go home and put it in your father's pipes and play to the strangers. Then they shall see that report said not enough of the music of the Macintyres." For the pretty little lady was jealous for the fame of her lover's family.

The young man did as she told him. He went home, and there, sure enough, were the strangers being hospitably entertained with food and drink after their journey from far lands. After they had eaten, and while they were resting, the lad said to his father that he would now take the pipes and amuse the strangers who had come home to them from over the waves. "You play!" said the father; "you could never play anything in your life—you will just cause us to be laughed at." The young man however prepared the pipes and put in the fairy reed, and he played the music that astonished every one. His family listened with surprise and delight, and the strangers were without speech. They had never heard or dreamt of such nobly sweet music—music which spoke to their souls and told them good and great things that they had never felt before in the world. It seemed not of earth, so sweet and strange it was. And the lad did it so simply—he just blew as usual, and he moved his fingers with no more trouble than any one else, yet he played fast, loud, joyful music, and slow, solemn, sorrowful music. It was like the music of "Tir nan Og"—the Land of the Ever-young.

After he stopped playing his listeners sat silent for a long space, for they could not speak. But when the spell left them and the strangers' speech came back, they whispered to each other that none dared compete against that, and that they themselves must not touch the pipes. So, as it was the mannerly custom among the Gaels to invite strangers to show their skill, they soon took leave of Macintyre and his family, for it was considered rude to refuse to play when asked. After they had, with much pretended hurry, bid good health be with their entertainers, they hastened to their coracle and sailed away out of that, saying to each other, "If that is what the lad does who, they say, cannot play, what can the old man's music be?" and they returned no more to South Uist, for they themselves were known musicians—but they had no fairy reed or chanter!

—by E. C. Carmichael, from *The Celtic Review* (Volume II: July 1905–April 1906). Originally titled "Never Was Piping So Sad, And Never Was Piping So Gay."

—❖—

One Midsummer's Eve, when the Bel-fires were lighted,
And the bag-piper's tone call'd the maidens delighted,
I joined a gay group by the Araglin's water,
And danced till the dawn with O'Donovan's daughter.
From the traditional song "O'Donovan's Daughter"

Bagpipes versus Fiddle

I' the haugh where the Don rins by bonny Braidha',
In a cot i' the clachan dwelt Murdo Macraw,
Weel kent far an' near as a frolicsome blade—
A Piper for sport, and a Thatcher by trade.

There wasna a cliack, a dancin', or fair,
A weddin' or christ'nin', but Murdo was there;
Wi' his pipes an' his drones he wad baith skirl an' blaw—
An' muckle requested was Murdo Macraw.

To neighbourin' farmers in hairst he wad shear—
He could trap hares an' rabbits, or sawmon could spear;
Brak dogs for the huntin' o' otters an' brocks,
Or fettle at guns, either barrels or locks.

He made rods for fishin', an' twistit their lines—
The lasses lo'ed Murdo, and he lo'ed the queans;
Nae ane in particular, he courtit them a'—
They were whiles like to fecht about Murdo Macraw.

An affair that occurr'd gied his credit a shog;
To Braidha' came a Wricht a' the way frae Drumclog—
A canty wee chiel, wha could handle the bow,
At the new country dances, like Donald or Gow.

Country dances were now a' the rage o' the day,
An' Murdo could play but a reel or strathspey;
Sae seldom if ever be now got a ca'—
'T is a cursed piece o' business, thocht Murdo Macraw.

The hairst was ta'en in, and the rucks got a hap—
The fodder was lang, an' a bountiful crap;
I' the gloamin' the Greive stappit o'er to the Wricht,
As the cliack was to be on the Wednesday nicht.

But after the lads an' the lasses were met,
Ye needna misdoot that they a' lookit blate,
For somehow the Wricht through the day gaed awa—
They had nae ither help but seek Murdo Macraw.

Macraw thocht a slur on his pipes had been cast,
He demurr'd for a while, but consentit at last;
The pipes were ta'en down, an' he dress'd himsel' braw—
Ye may judge sic a welcome he got at Braidha'.

He scarcely had played twa strathspeys to the ear,
When the canty wee Fiddler cam in wi' a steer;
The fiddle was straikit wi' mony a "ha, ha!"
An' few tint a thocht upon Murdo Macraw.

The supper was owre, an' the lasses were fain
To be on the floor at the dancin' again;
But ye ken disappointments is ilka ane's lot —
The fiddle was lost, an' it couldna be got.

They lookit the "but" an' ransackit the "ben,"
But nae ane could guess whare the fiddle was gane.
Then they cried for the pipes—they were also awa';
"They are after the fiddle," said Murdo Macraw.

Says Forbes the Greive, "'T is remarkable queer
How bagpipes an' fiddle should baith disappear;
First married who gets them"—when, strange-like to tell,
They were found 'neath the barm in a tubfu' o' ale.

They drew out the fiddle, completely a wrack,
The Wricht lookit gloomy, tho' naething he spak;
Nae waur was the pipes, wi' a squeeze an' a blaw—
"Tak ye that for your fiddlin'," thocht Murdo Macraw.

—by William Anderson, *Rhymes, Reveries, and Reminiscences,* 1867.

Turlough MacSweeney

Turlough MacSweeney (1831–1916) was an accomplished piper and fiddler whose ancestors were of the royal line of Ireland. Francis O'Neill (see page 23), who met MacSweeney when he performed at the 1893 Chicago World's Fair, wrote of the encounter in his book Irish Minstrels and Musicians: *"For an Irish piper his coldness and reticence were in marked contrast with the manners of most persons of his class. This taciturnity may have been constitutional, yet who knows it may be the visible effects of maintaining the dignity of a distinguished piper, conscious of his descent from the chieftains of the once powerful Clan Mac Suibhne of Tír Chonaill."*

A health to you, Piper,
    And your pipes silver-tongued,
clear and sweet in their crooning!

Full of the music they gathered at morn
    On your high heather hills from the lark on the wing,
From the blackbird at eve on the blossoming thorn,
    From the little green linnet whose plaining they sing,
And the joy and the hope in the heart of the Spring,
        O, Turlough MacSweeney!

Play us our Eire's most sorrowful songs,
    As she sits by her reeds near the wash of the wave,
That the coldest may thrill at the count of her wrongs,
    That the sword may flash forth from the scabbard to save,
And the wide land awake at the wrath of the brave,
        O, Turlough MacSweeney!

Play as the bards played in days long ago,
    When O'Donnell, arrayed for the foray or feast,
With your kinsmen from Bannat and Fannat and Doe,
    With piping and harping, and blessing of priest,

Rode out in the blaze of the sun from the East,
      O, Turlough MacSweeney!

Play as they played in that rapturous hour
   When the clans heard in gladness his young fiery call
Who burst from the gloom of the Sassenach tower,
   And sped to the welcome in dear Donegal,
Then on to his hailing as chieftain of all—
      O, Turlough MacSweeney!

Play as they played, when, a trumpet of war,
   His voice for the rally, pealed up to the blue,
And the kerns from the hills and the glens and the scaur
   Marched after the banner of conquering Hugh—
Led into the fray by a piper like you,
      O, Turlough MacSweeney!

And surely no note of such music shall fail,
   Wherever the speech of our Eire is heard,
To foster the hope of the passionate Gael,
   To fan the old hatred, relentless when stirred,
To strengthen our souls for the strife to be dared,
      O, Turlough MacSweeney!

May your pipes, silver-tongued, clear and sweet in their crooning,
   Keep the magic they captured at dawning and even
From the blackbird at home, and the lark on its journey,
   From the thrush on its spray, and the little green linnet.
     A health to you, Piper!

        —From *The Four Winds of Eirinn* by Ethna Carbery
     (Anna MacManus), edited by Seumas MacManus, 1913.

The Piper Came to Our Town

Turlough and the Fairy King

Turlough MacSweeney was not always a gifted piper. Despairing of other means of attaining success, it occurred to him to make an appeal to the fairies on the rath of Gaeth-Doir. One moonlight night, he plucked up courage, and with his pipes buckled on all ready for playing, he made his way up along the boreen and across the fields and timidly entered the fort. Here, in his own words, is the tale as he told it to Francis O'Neill. It is found in Irish Minstrels and Musicians.

Well, as I was saying, when I got to the center of the Plasog, as near as I could tell, you may be sure I wasn't any too comfortable. Anyhow, I addressed myself to the king of the fairies, saying: 'I'm Turlogh McSweeney, the piper of Gwedore, and I hope you will pardon my boldness for coming to ask your majesty to play a chune on the pipes for me, and I'll return the compliment and play for you.' Yerra, man, like a shot out of a gun, the words were hardly out of my mouth when the grandest music of many pipers, let alone one, playing all together, filled my ears; and that wasn't all, for lo and behold you, what should I see but scores of little fairies or *luricanns*, wearing red caps, neatly footing it, as if for a wager. Believe me, I was so overcome with fright at such a strange and unexpected sight that I ran for the bare life, my pipes hanging to me and dropping off piece and joint along the way; and by the time I reached home, the dickens a bit of my whole set of pipes was left to me but the bellows and bag, and they couldn't let go, as they were strapped round my waist.

Picture to yourselves the kind of a night I spent after what happened. Anyway, by sun-up in the morning I ventured out and started to try and pick up the disjointed sections of my pipes, as I knew well enough the route I ran. My luck relieved my misgivings when I found the last missing part, which had dropped off at the very entrance to the rath or fort when I ran away.

I lost no time in putting the now complete instrument in order, and to keep my word and fulfil my promise made to the king of the fairies the night before, I struck up 'The Wild Irishman,' my favorite reel. Words can't express my astonishment and delight when I found I could play as well as the best of them. And that, gentlemen, is how I came to be the best Union piper of my day in that part of the country.

Many years after that, when I was living alone in the little cabin after my mother died—God rest her soul—there came to the door in the dusk of the evening a stranger and nothing less than a piper, by the way, who with a 'God save all here,' introduced himself as was customary. I invited him in, of course, and after making himself at aise he says, 'Would you like to hear a 'chune' on the pipes?' 'I would that,' said I, for you know a piper and his music are always welcome in an Irish home. Taking his pipes out of the bag, he laid them on the bed beside him, and what do you think but without anyone laying a finger on them, they struck up 'Toss the Feathers' in a way that would make a cripple get up and dance. After a while, when they stopped, he says, 'Will you play a 'chune' for me now?' I said I would and welcome, pulling the blanket off my pipes that were hid under the bedclothes, to keep the reeds from drying out. 'Give us *Seaghan ua Dmbhir an Gleanna*' (Shaun O'Dheir an Glanna), says I to the pipes, and when they commenced to play, the mysterious stranger, who no doubt was a fairy, remarked, 'Ah! Mac, I see you are one of us.' With that, both sets of pipes played half a dozen 'chimes' together. When they had enough of it, the fairy picked up his pipes and put them in the green bag again. If I had any doubts about him before, I had none at all when he said familiarly, 'Mac, I'm delighted with my visit here this evening, and as I have several other calls to make I'll have to be after bidding you good night, but if I should happen to be passing this way again, I'll be sure to drop in.'

—From *Irish Minstrels and Musicians* by Francis O'Neill, 1913.

The Piper Came to Our Town

The Pipers o' Buchan

Respectfu', renowned bagbrethren,
    Wha sells a puff wind by retail;
Gae hearken to ane o' your kettren,—
    I in your commodity deal.
My gypsie sall try a' her cheepers,
    Her belts an' her win-breads put on,
And teen to the praise o' Scotch Pipers,
    Her chanter, reeds, burdens and drone.

Agreeable to history we're ancient,
    And honourable our pedigree;
By Moses ye ken we are mentioned,
    Fan ilk ane had lan' that was free.
Ere aul Tubal Cain's plumb-jordon
    Had clinket a rivet upon,
Young Tubal had tun'd up his burden,
    Was liltin at 'Clout the caldron'.

Whan David was young, wi' his tykie
    He herdit his sheep on a ley;
At the sun-sheenie-side o' a dykie
    The laddie first learnt to play.
Fan Saul was sere vext wi' a devil,
    He ca'd him to play by his throne,
Auld nick got a charge o' remeval,
    He scar'd him to hell wi' his Drone.

Fan Amphion, that famous piper,
    Was biggin the Thebean Wa',
He needit nae hewer nor cutter,
    Nae horses the fowdrie to ca'.
For after him trees came in dances,
    And tumble on tumble ilk stone,

Syne biggit strong ramparts and fences,
    And a' by the sound o' his Drone.

Whan aul piper Orpheus married
    His beautiful bride, Euridice,
By a lecherous diel she was carried
    Straught aff to hell in a trice.
Th' aul piper he begg'd to restore her,
    Wi' mony sad sigh and Ohon,
But naething the diel wad tak for her,
    Yet tremblin, he dreadit the Drone!

Soon as his liburnims he soundit,
    He rais'd sic an uproar in hell,
The harpies and furies confundit,
    Broke ilka enchantment and spell.
Even Ixion's wheel wudna turn him,
    Nor Sysiphus tumble his stone,
Sic power had his matchless liburnims
    Sic magical charms had his Drone.

Radamanthus and Pluto consentit
    To grant the aul piper his boon,
Proserpine sternly relentit.
    And gave him, for life, his drug-down.
He play'd Cerberus th' porter asleep,
    Then Pluto he bade him begone,
He awa wi' the carline did creep,
    And cuddom'd his wife wi' his Drone.

We are aye well loo'd by the lasses,
    In dizens and scores they'll convene,
They're sure o' maurdell o' kisses,
    Fan they get a dance o' the green.
Some cries, play us up 'Sleepy Maggy',
    'Tail Toddle,' or 'Nancy does yon;'

And some seeks the 'Best o' the Baggie',
  And dances like daft to our Drone.

Ye'll hear the young wenches conferrin
  Wi' aul Auntie Bess at her wheel,
Their joes and their sweet-hearts comparin,
  And wha has the lover maist leal.
Quo Jeannie, I like my dear Jamie,
  (But telling this secret to none,)
For ilka time he comes to see me,
  I aye get a spring on his Drone.

Quo Nelly, my piper's my Jewel,
  Luve burns at my heart like a coal,
Sae neatly he handles the tewel,
  His fingers sae sweet on the hole.
It's happiness to me to hear him
  Play 'O'er the green meadows alone',
But oh I am blest whan I'm near him,
  Whan o'er my lap he lays his Drone!

Quo Betty, I mean not to tarry,
  For I've made a promise and vow,
My piper, my sodger, I'll marry,
  For I like the red and the blue.
Then I'll get the knapsack to carry,
  Sae merrily as we'll march on;
There's naething like the military,
  To follow the drum and the Drone.

Hear me, says aul Bessie, their auntie,
  I've liv'd wi' my piper, it's true,
O' simmers and winters these twenty,
  And never had cause yet to rue.
He's well-worth his room in the pantry,
  He ne'er gae me reason to moan,

He's fed me fu' well wi' his chauntrie,
　　And gard me gie braw wi' his Drone.

We are honest in our occupation,
　　It lies na in our way to cheat,
It's 'gainst the laws o' our profession
　　To seek ony mair than we get.
But gin ony gen'rous fellows
　　Their bountith bestow us upon,
Our gratitude blows like our bellows.
　　We soun forth their praise wi' our Drone.

We deavna the house wi' state-matters,
　　Whan we're at our pint or our gill,
But wha best pinches and barters,
　　And wha o' reed-makin has skill.
We fashna our head wi' the banters
　　Tweesh Prelate and Presbyter John,
But buyin and nifferin o' chanters,
　　And teenin, and soundin our Drone.

Our lug and our finger exact is,
　　To measure our time and our rest,
The theory wantin the practice,
　　Is stark-staring nonsense at best.
Our thumb has the knack o' transposing,
　　Or shifting o' the semitone,
We play to the key at the closing,
　　And symphony souns wi' our Drone.

Our brave highlan heroes it charms,
　　When their martial pibrochs they hear,
Their matchless achievements in arms,
　　Keeps a' the wide warld in fear.
How mony strong forts hae they storm'd,
　　How mony fierce battles they've won,

What wonders hae they not perform'd,
  Inspired by the sons o' the Drone?

Now join in a toast to Scotch pipers,
  A piper, you see, is a knabb,
Come then lat us teen up our cheepers,
  Our honour swells up like our bag.
Our company's welcome to princes,
  By the rangel we're doated upon,
For gladness their verra heart dances,
  To hear the sweet chanter and Drone.

—From *Gleanings of Scotch, English, and Irish Scarce Old Ballads*
by Peter Buchan, 1825.

In the notes to the original, Buchan writes: As depicted in the ballad, our national music has charms in the hands of our brave countrymen, to cheer the wounded and dying hero. Out of hundreds of anecdotes that could be produced, I shall only give the following: The Piper of the 71st regiment, being severely wounded at the battle of Vimeira, in 1809, was unable to keep his legs, but this did not damp his military ardour, for raising himself on the ground he called out, "I canna gang farther wi' you, lads, but deil hae' my saul if ye shall want music;" and he continued to animate them with his most warlike airs.

—❖—

They sent for a fiddler and piper to play,
They danced and they sung until the break of day,
Then Jack to his hammock with Betsy did go,
While the fiddler and the piper played "Rosin, the beau,"
From the Traditional Ballad "Sale of a Wife"

The Wounded Piper
of Elandslaagte

The Battle of Elandslaagte was a battle of the Second Boer War (1899–1902), fought between the British Empire and two independent Boer republics, the South African Republic and the Orange Free State. The war ended with the Treaty of Vereeniging, placing the republics in the British Empire. The newly created Union of South Africa, predecessor to the current Republic of South Africa, became part of the Commonwealth in 1910.

You know the way the Gordons fought at Elandslaagte Hill,
How they charged the blazing kopje[1], how they cheered;
How the pipes were always skirling with a Gordon piper's will
Till the laagers[2] and the rifle-pits were cleared.

There are lassies o'er the Border who are weeping sore to-day
For the flowers of bonnie Scotland lost and dead;
For the lads of our own Highlands on those highlands cast away
By the foemen and their torrent-rain of lead.

There is one brave Highland piper who is sad as sad can be,
Just to think his pipes had played no victor's part;
And this is what the piper of the Gordons told to me,
When I found him after battle out of heart.

"Well, you see, I had no business to be playing at the front;
Little use in showing Doctor such an arm;
'Serve you right, man,' he would answer, he is straight as he is blunt;
'Keep your pipes behind the boulders out of harm.'

"I hardly felt the bullet, tho' my pipes were drenched with blood;
Was I going out of action like a girl?

1. A small hill rising up from the African veld.
2. A camp defended by a circular formation of wagons.

The Piper Came to Our Town

So I took a dead man's shirt and tore it strip-wise where I stood,
Bound the wound up tight and finished out the skirl.

"Finished out and played another,
cocked the reeds and let them drone,
Gave the bag a clip the tighter as I blew.
They shall pay for it, and dearly shall they hear the time and tune!
And with gallant Gordons round me, on I flew.

"Oh the rattle of the Maxim![3] Oh the live shells screaming o'er!
Oh the cry, 'What price Majuba!'[4] Oh the shout!
If I live to be a hundred I shall not forget the roar,
As we stormed the ridge to turn the foemen out.

"I played what Gordons love most, and my bag of wind was full,
When, bayonets all aflame, the ridge we topped;
And I thought I still was playing, then there came a moment's lull,
And I listened and I heard the pipes had stopped.

"They—my brand-new Edinboro' pipes, with Gordon colours grand!
And a hole right through my bag of Highland breath!
If you never won a battle, sir, you scarce can understand,
But I almost wish that ball had been my death.

"It's not the bullet thro' my arm that makes me sad to-day—
With bone unbroke the wound will soon be right;
I am down at heart for thinking that my pipes just ceased to play
When the Boers at Elandslaagte turned to flight."

—From *Ballads of the War* by Hardwicke Drummond Rawnsley
with a prefatory note by Arthur Conan Doyle, 1901.

---

3. A single-barreled, water-cooled machine gun named for inventor Sir Hiram
S. Maxim (1840-1916).
4. Refers to the Battle of Majuba Hill, a victory for the Boers.

The Piper Came to Our Town   223

Prisoner of War
Friedberg, November 1, 1917

Even pipers did, on occasion, fall into the hands of the enemy and were seldom allowed to take their instruments with them into captivity. However, some officers, like this man from the Gordon Highlanders, were allowed to keep theirs. In some internment camps pipe bands formed with as many as a dozen pipers.

Though only a young piper, I play here every day and do not find people too hostile to me. The Russians, French and even the Germans greet me with great interest and seem to find pleasure in listening to me—though as I said I am no great player. The most unsympathetic are always to be found among the ranks of the "Sassanach". I learnt to play in 1911, on joining my regiment, under George MacLennan, who was pipe-major at that time. While on leave in Edinburgh I used to have lessons with his father—Jno. MacLennan. Up till now I have only attempted "The Glen is Mine" and "Struan Robertson" in Piobaireachd, but having been thoroughly taught by the MacLennans, I naturally follow their way of thinking. Yesterday I played to a Russian who is a very good player of the piano. He was delighted with the Pipes and I could not play too many tunes for him. Strathspeys and Reels are greatly appreciated by all our Russian friends. Last St. Andrew's Day we organized an Exhibition of dancing which was a complete success. As the Scottish Colony here is so small we asked the Russians to come and help us. This they did right well with dances and songs, the music being provided, in both cases, by "Balalaika", the Russian national instrument. For our part we danced two foursome Reels (dancing two different sets of steps), a Sword Dance and a Highland Schottische. In the latter dance we took a Russian as a partner, they having been trained up for the event. We sang "Bonnie Dundee", "Lassies of Scotland", "MacPherson", and finished up with "Auld Lang Syne". For the Reels my Russian friend provided the music on the piano.

Our costume was of course improvised. Kilt, shoes and hose we had, we wore white shirts with lace cuffs, a strip of tartan fastened with a brooch at the shoulder to do duty as a plaid and a black velvet band with lace ruffle, falling down in front, round our necks. Our sporans, with the exception of one which was made of a local rabbit, all came from home. I had several pretty compliments paid to me by the Russians and French, both on our costumes and dancing. Five of us took part altogether. I wonder if it would be too much to ask you to send me instructions for dancing the "Lochaber Broadswords" and the "Seann Triubhas", in case we have the misfortune to pass another St. Andrew's Day here in Germany. If we do we shall give another exhibition and I would like to be able to vary it. I only know 12 Strathspey steps and eight Reel steps. Since I have been prisoner I have taught 30 people to dance the Reel—including two Frenchmen and one Russian, and at present I have five pupils on the chanter. We are 16 Scots here, so can you say we are losing our national distinctions? I have only told you this because I thought it would interest you.

—From *The pipes of war: a record of the achievements of pipers of Scottish and overseas regiments during the war, 1914–18,* by Bruce Gordon Seton, John Grant, Neil Munro, Boyd Cable, and Philip Gibbs, 1920.

— ❖ —

*The Irish gave the bagpipes to the Scots as a joke,
but the Scots haven't got the joke yet.*
Oliver Herford

The Kirk of Killiechrist

In the early part of the 17th century, Angus, eldest son of Glengarry...
was intercepted by a...band of Mackenzies, and slain with a number of
his followers... A party of Glengarry's men were sent, under the com-
mand of Allan Mac Raonuill of Lundy, to revenge his death. Allan led
them into the parish of Urray, in Ross shire, on a Sunday morning, and
surprised a numerous body of the Mackenzies assembled at prayer
within the walls of Cillie-christ... Allan gave orders to set the build-
ing on fire. The miserable victims...were, without a single exception—
man, woman, and child—swallowed up by the devouring element, or
indiscriminately massacred by the swords of the relentless Macdonells,
whilst a piper marched round the church, playing an extemporary
piece of music, which has ever since been the pibroch of the Glengarry
family. —From "Guide to the Highlands," The Monthly Review, 1834.

The kirk was filled on Sunday morn,
  The kirk of Killiechrist,
When down the glen Glengarry's men
  Came swarming through the mist,
And rent the air with joyful yell
To find the foeman snared so well,
And drowned the psalm with savage din,
And mocked the wail that rose within.
With dirk and sword they hacked the boughs,
  And heaped the heather round,
They lit the fire, and fanned it higher
  With scarf and plaid unbound,
And laughed with hellish glee, to hear
The prisoned wail of woe and fear,
And gashed the writhing hands that tore
At window-chink, and guarded door.
"The piper, ho!" Macdonald cried,
  And forth the piper sprang,
And hitched and hove and strained and strove
  Till drone and chanter sang.

"Now," said the chief, with wicked glance,
"We'll give them music to their dance,
And you shall earn a silver crown,
When you have played the dancers down."
The piper marched around the kirk,
    The kirk of Killiechrist—
High rose in air the smoke and glare,
    The faggots cracked and hissed;
The fierce flames shot with hungry roar
Through crackling roof and crumbling door,
And licked with red and ravening tongue
The shuddering prey on which they sprung.
But round and round the piper marched
    With puffed and purple face,
And tuned his drones to chiming tones,
    And timed his stately pace.
And now the death-shriek louder wailed,
And now the screaming pipe prevailed,
Now bag-pipe lilt and wild lament
In one infernal chorus blent.
Down sank the roof, and upwards shot
    From out the crumbling crust,
A fiery stream, a bloody steam,
    A whirl of smoke and dust;
The smouldering rafters piled the floor,
Where shriek and moan were heard no more,
And, rent with many a yawning crack,
The ghastly walls stood bare and black.
The piper marched around the kirk,
    The kirk of Killiechrist,
And tuned his drones to louder tones
    With many a turn and twist.
And from his pipe a blast he blew
Of yelling triumph wild and new,
The pibroch destined long to fan
The warfire of Glengarry's clan.
            —From *Ballads and Poems* by William Martin, 1879.

The Piper Came to Our Town

Hannaberry the Piper

The County Wexford, of all parts of Ireland, is peculiarly rich in legends, traditions and fairy tales. In former days, before the advent of the newspaper press and the national schoolmaster, there was not a district, town or village within its borders but boasted of its story-teller, who was generally the depository of all the marvelous and uncanny events that had taken place in the neighborhood for ages past. But in these days of railroads, telegraphs, schools and cheap literature, the long-honored tribe of story-tellers is disappearing, even in the County of Wexford. A few remain, however, to this day, but their occupation has fearfully fallen into desuetude. Some of them may still be found lingering around their old haunts at the glowing firesides of comfortable farmers, but many of them were swallowed up in that great stream of immigration that poor old Erin has been pouring on our American shores for the last half century. Of the latter was Jimmy Chili, who, though he bore a name that savored of South America, was as true a Wexfordian as ever danced a jig in New Ross, from which good old town he hailed.

I first became acquainted with Jimmy when he was a "youngster" in the ancient colony of Newfoundland. Like myself, he was then employed in the dangerous but profitable occupation of seal hunting. In the intervals of the hunt, and in the long winter nights, seated around the forecastle fire, he often beguiled the tedium of the flow passing hours with story, jest and song. Jimmy was a firm believer in witchcraft, ghosts, fairies, warnings, second sight, and all the mysteries which are supposed to hedge in the supernatural order. Whether he believed in his own tales or not I cannot say; but certain he always delivered himself of them, particularly when they related to ghosts and fairies, in such a solemn, oracular way, as to carry conviction to his hearers among the simple fishermen and seal hunters of Newfoundland. I well remember one night, after having made everything snug on deck, we were seated at the forecastle fire. After Jimmy had drank his tea, filled his pipe and smoked it, he was called upon for a story.

"Be gob, boys," said he in response, "I'll tell you the story of Hannaberry the Piper and the Marquis of Waterford. Hannaberry was the greatest piper in all the country around New Ross. Divil a marriage, christening, fair or wake widin' miles but he would be at wid his pipes, and thim were the pipes, don't be talking."

I will not attempt, however, to give the story verbatim in Jimmy's vernacular, but that was the opening sentence. What follows I shall relate as concisely as possible, and keeping as near the original text as I can.

"One night," Jimmy went on, "Hannaberry, who had been to the fair of Taghmon, which is situated between New Ross and Wexford town, was returning home, with his pipes, as usual, under his arm. He had passed a merry day of it, and, as a consequence, felt pretty much as Tam O'Shanter, of Scottish memory, felt when he pronounced himself victorious over all the ills of life. Down came Hannaberry, in this jolly mood, along the road to New Ross. From Taghmon to his home it was a goodly walk, and after the fatigues of the day it was only natural that he should feel a trifle tired. When he came to the old lime-kiln, that is exactly four miles from Ross bridge, he thought he would rest himself and have a pull at his old *dudheen*; 'twould refresh him and waken up his faculties, which were, in a manner, becoming oblivious. He had no sooner conceived the idea than he proceeded to carry it into execution by seating himself on the sloping ground that led to the top of the lime-kiln, lighting his pipe and commencing to smoke. Before seating himself he laid his beloved pipes carefully away in a nook of the kiln. He had not smoked long before a dreamy, drowsy, undefinable sensation crept over him. The smoke from his pipe appeared to resolve itself into a mysterious halo of light, which gradually began to enshroud him. Suddenly he heard the most delicious strains of music proceeding from a short distance behind where he was seated. Never had such strains been produced on Irish pipes as Hannaberry now listened to, and turning, he beheld a sight which struck him with awe and astonishment. Coming towards him, with the pipes under his arm, was a little, a very little, old man, nattily dressed in green. The little old man handled the pipes with the most consummate skill and grace, and, standing before the astonished Hannaberry, he played twelve of the most delightful and patriotic airs in a style the most lovely and bewitching. When he had ceased playing he laid down the pipes, and, fixing a pair of piercing black eyes on the bewildered piper, addressed him thus:

"'Why, then, Mick Hannaberry, it's yourself that's a brave man, by daring to sit down so comfortably in a fairy rath. I have been here now bordering on five hundred years, and you are the first man that has had the courage to cross the magic ring and rest himself in my domains. And now, me man, let me tell you that you have conferred a favor on me that shall not go unrewarded.'

"When the little old man in green had stopped speaking, he lifted the pipes from the ground, and placing them under Hannaberry's arm, he ordered the now fairly bewildered piper to strike up a tune. Hannaberry at first was very timid and bashful, particularly after hearing such beautiful music from the fairy, as he now fully knew him to be. He pleaded weariness and inability, but the little old man with a quiet dignity awed, while at the same time he reassured, the piper into a compliance with his demand, and Mick Hannaberry struck up a jig so lively and soul-stirring, that the performer himself was completely surprised at the delicacy and proficiency with which he handled the keys of his instrument.

"Tune after tune, to the number of twelve, was rattled off on the pipes, by the now thoroughly delighted piper, who already began to congratulate himself on the great advantage his increased proficiency in his art would give him over his less fortunate rivals, who had never stumbled into a fairy rath to become acquainted with its occult mysteries. The little man in green eyed the piper all the while with the keenest and shrewdest glances, apparently reading the thoughts that were uppermost in his mind.

"'Be aisy, now, Mick,' said he, 'and lay down the pipes till I explain. As I said afore, yours is the first mortal face of a piper that I have set eyes on in this sacred ring for five hundred years.'

"'Be gorra, then, that's a long time, your honor,' said Mick in reply, looking out curiously from under the rim of his old hat at the little old man in green, and wondering all the while what was coming next.

"'Yes, five hundred weary years have I been imprisoned here, till this blessed night, when some good chance has sent you to my relief. And Mick, me man, I'll forever bless the day you came to relieve me, besides assisting you to make your fortune.'

"'It's thankful I am to your honor,' replied Mick, still feeling not quite at ease, and wishing in his heart that he was safely at home with the old woman and children.

"'There is a condition, however,' said the little old man in green, 'and, unfortunately, one that cannot be dispensed with. It is inseparable from my unfortunate position, and in many respects will counterbalance the great benefit conferred upon you. When you leave here to-night your fame will be abroad through all the country; indeed, it will not be confined to poor old Ireland, but will be spread throughout the whole of the three kingdoms. Your services will be in great request. Your pipes, by merely placing them on a table, will be operated upon by an unseen agency, and the most delicious music will be produced; but,' and here the little old man's face assumed a grave aspect, '*every time the pipes are played you will lose a near relative by death.* This is the inevitable condition, which you must either accept or remain with me until another piper comes to your relief and mine. Five hundred years ago, when in the flesh, like you, I was a piper. I wasted my days in mirth, joviality and song. I was idle and encouraged idleness in others, and as a punishment for my thoughtless conduct, I was condemned to pass ages in the narrow confines of this rath. I was to be freed, however, when a man of my own profession would voluntarily come within the magic circle which surrounds my limited domains. It has been your fortune to be the man, and whether that fortune is to be good or evil for you your future conduct will tell. Take your pipes, you are now at liberty to go; but do not forget the penalty that is attached to your music, and remember,

The Piper Came to Our Town   231

also, you must never refuse a reasonable request for your services as a piper.'

"The halo of light gradually faded away, and the dazed Hannaberry found himself cold, benumbed and damp, his pipes beside him, and still seated on the side of the little mound that led to the top of the lime kilns. He rubbed his eyes and wondered if it was not all a dream, and if he had not taken too much whisky, and whether the little old man in green and the music was not a phantom of a disordered brain. But no, it must have been a reality; for there, sure enough, was the fairy ring all around him, and no true Irish piper could ever doubt the evidence of his senses, when he was environed by so palpable a fact as that.

"With many misgivings and doubts he got up and started for his home, and the way he put himself over the ground between the old lime kiln and Ross bridge was wonderful to behold. The next morning, bright and early, before Hannaberry was awake, a well-to-do farmer from a neighboring district was after him to come and play at his daughter's wedding, which was about to take place. With the recollection of the scenes of last night still fresh in his mind, the poor piper faltered and hesitated for some time. The farmer wondered at his reluctance, and at his mysterious and absent manner. Such conduct was unusual in Hannaberry, and the farmer thought he would try what effect a glass or two would have upon him. In Hannaberry's depressed condition the whisky worked a magic charm. After imbibing he at once recovered his assurance and old sprightliness and promised to attend the wedding of the farmer's daughter on the following night.

"And sure enough, when the guests assembled at the farmer's at the appointed time, there was the piper with his pipes promptly on hand. When he made his appearance in the dancing-room, he placed his pipes on the table, and went to congratulate the new-married pair. In the meantime the lads and lasses had ranged themselves on the floor in sets for the dance, and the word went around, 'Strike up the music, Hannaberry!' No sooner had the request been made, than the pipes on the table commenced to play the most beautiful dancing tunes that had ever been heard in

The Piper Came to Our Town

those parts. Hannaberry was as much astonished at first as any of the company; but by a powerful effort of the will he controlled his emotions, muttering only to himself, 'Be gorra, I am an enchanted man, surely.' The dancers turned to the piper for an explanation, charging him with witchcraft, the black art, and all other kinds of magic. Determined to make the best of a bad job, and now perfectly self-possessed, Hannaberry replied, 'Be aisy now, boys; sure it's only a new invention of me own in the musical line. Sarra a thing yez need do but dance, and I'll furnish the music. Dance away, and never a hair of yer head will be hurt.' His coolness reassured them, his advice was good, the music was better, the guests in good humor, and so on the light fantastic toe they tripped the merry hours away until the dawning of another day.

"When poor Hannaberry returned home in the morning, a new and sad revelation broke in upon him. His mother-in-law, stark and stiff, lay dead in the house. His wife informed him that about midnight the family Banshee had set up the death-cry in the garden behind the house; that shortly after her mother was taken suddenly faint, and gave up the ghost in a short time, before a doctor or any other person could be called to her assistance. This was a stunning blow to the piper. Of what use was the great gift of musical proficiency if, on every occasion it was exercised, he was to lose a near and dear relative? For, strange as it may appear, he really loved his mother-in-law.

"But as the little old man in green had predicted, Hannaberry's fame spread over all Ireland. It was the theme of conversation in all circles high and low. At last it came to the ears of the Marquis of Waterford, who was at that time the leading sporting man in all Ireland. The marquis was well known as the greatest betting man of his day, and on a certain evening after dinner, in conversation with his guests, English and Scotch noblemen, he boldly asserted that Mick Hannaberry was the greatest piper in all the three kingdoms. Of course no patriotic English or Scotch nobleman could admit this. The marquis, however, insisted on the truth of his assertion, and offered to back it up by staking the whole of his immense estates on the issue of a contest with the pipes between Hannaberry and any other piper that England or Scotland could produce. His challenge was instantly accepted by an English nobleman, who stipulated that the trial of skill should come off in London, before the Court and all the nobility.

"The next day the marquis sought out Hannaberry, and told him what he had done. The poor piper had not yet forgotten the mysterious death of his mother-in-law, and in consequence received the proposal of the marquis to go to London to play rather coolly. 'Hannaberry,' said the marquis, 'the best farm on my estate shall be given to you and yours while grass grows and water runs, if you come with me to London; and besides, man, isn't my whole estate bet upon you, and for the honor of old Ireland, surely, you would not see me deprived of my estates by the bluff of any Englishman that ever lived?'

"This fervent appeal settled the question, and Hannaberry agreed to accompany the marquis to London to test the skill of the best English and Scotch pipers. The next day the marquis, with the piper and a large retinue, set out for London, where they arrived in due time. The scene of the trial of skill was to be in the palace court-yard, before the Queen and all the highest nobility of the land.

"When the great day arrived, pipers from England and Scotland, including the Duke of Argyle's own piper, were on hand to contest the marquis' claim for the championship of Hannaberry. The poor fellow himself felt somewhat abashed when he stepped into the arena with his pipes, but the recollection of the little old man in green cheered him up. Seated around in a vast amphitheatre was the Queen, Prince Albert, the Duke of Wellington, and all the other great nobles of the land, arrayed in the most dazzling uniforms it was possible to imagine.

"Out from the gaily-dressed crowd stepped the Marquis of Waterford, and called for a table. It was brought instantly, and Hannaberry placed the pipes upon it. Moved by the unseen agency of the fairies, the pipes struck up and produced the most ravishing music, to the astonishment and delight of the vast audience. After the twelve tunes were played in grand style, the marquis stepped out and said: 'Show me the man in England or Scotland that can bate that.'

"'The divil a man in England or Scotland either,' said the Duke of Wellington, 'that can bate that, and it's proud I am this day—yis, as proud as I was the day I bate the French at Waterloo—that a countryman of mine can take the shine out of the whole world on the pipes. Be off home with you now, Hannaberry, and good luck to you; and, marquis, mind you treat him well.'

"'Be dad, I'll do that same,' replied the marquis. And he did; for on their return to Ireland he settled, as he had promised, the finest farm on his estate on the victorious piper, whose good fortune was rather dampened, however, when he was told that his uncle and his aunt, too, had died at the very time the shouts of victory were going up for him from the aristocracy in London.

"He never played the pipes after that, and, for all I know, he still lives on the same farm," said Jimmy Chili, as he lit his pipe and went on deck to take his trick at the wheel.

—From *The Zozimus Papers: A Series of Comic and Sentimental Stories and Legends, Being the Edited, Unedited, and Pilfered Works of Michael Moran, the Blind Story-Teller of Dublin*, edited by P. J. Kennedy, 1889.

— ❖ —

There is a rath in the Queen's County, only four yards in diameter, but held so sacred as the fairies' dancing ground that no one dared to remove a handful of earth from the mound; and at night the sweetest low music may be heard floating round the hill, as if played by silver bagpipes.
From *Ancient Legends* by Lady Jane Wilde, 1888.

Music, Dancing and Drunkenness

There was a consecration-festival held in the neighborhood, and the music and dancing continued far into the night. But when the stars, brightly sparkling, and the moon high in heaven warned the revellers that it was time to break up, the inhabitants of the different villages joined company, and took their way homewards.

The village lasses wore pewter rings on their fingers, which their friends had given them at the fair, and the jovial village lads went on before, singing at the top of their voices. But their merriment was at its greatest height when Leonard was one of the party.

Leonard was the merriest and the most famous piper in that part of the world; he never knew what it was to be out of spirits, he played up at every dance, and he was always the most pleased of the whole party. Whenever there was a dance or a wedding he always came down from the mountains with his bagpipe, and he would play the livelong night.

He was never tired of playing, but he was also never tired of drinking; and if it had not been for the sake of his music, people would not always have been so glad to see him, for when he had drank a great deal, according to his usual custom, he became insufferable, for he did nothing but rave and swear.

At these times he would swear by all that was dear that he would remain a merry bagpiper till his end, and if he ever felt that he was going to die, he would drink deep, as long as he could, and mock death with the last wail of his bagpipe.

He had gone on with his usual recklessness on this occasion, or, if possible, he had been even wilder and more jovial than ever. Warning and persuasion were of no avail. "Leonard, beware for your own sake," his friends cried, in vain. He cursed and swore high and dry that he would die drunk, and in the midst of music and dancing, and not otherwise.

This time he preceded the homeward-bound troop. His bagpipe squeaked and whistled all the way, and the lads sang in their Swiss fashion, and the white dresses of the lasses glimmered in the moonlight.

When they came to the cross-way, where the roads parted, the bagpiper took the right-hand road, which led up to the heights.

The maidens stopped short and shrieked out, "Where are you going, piper? Here, the left-hand road, that goes round through the valley!"

Leonard pointed to the right, where the tower of the village church could be seen in the moonlight.

"Shall we not go this way?" he asked. "I thought it was nearer over the heath; why should we go so much out of our way?"

The maidens replied, "It is not safe to go over the heath, bagpiper; the dwarfs haunt the place in the night, and it is very seldom anyone passes over the heath in the night-time without getting into trouble."

Leonard burst into a hearty laugh. "Pray, what harm can the dwarfs do to anybody?"

"They force you to dance, and they can do you great harm."

"Ha! ha!" laughed Leonard again. "I have wandered about alone many a night, over mountain and valley, over cross-ways and even by the gallows, but nothing has ever happened to me yet. I should like right well to meet with the little people, for they are said to own a great deal of silver and gold, and it would be no bad thing if I filled my knapsack full. Where is the way to the dwarfs?"

"Leonard! Leonard!" cried the maidens, "be not so foolhardy; he who plunges headlong into danger only rushes upon his fate. If you go to the dwarfs, you'll have to dance till your breath is wholly gone."

"Dance?" replied Leonard. "That's just what I should like. Pray, have the little people any musicians to play for them?"

"They have the wind that whistles over the heath for their piper, and the night-birds join their songs by way of accompaniment."

"They cannot dance very well to such music as that; the little people ought to know for once how well one can dance by a bagpipe. Farewell, if you will not go with me. I'm going over the heath."

With these words he seized his bagpipe, played up a merry tune, and strode boldly up the heights which led to the heath.

The maidens and their companions raised a loud, lamenting cry, and hastened away.

Leonard strode fearlessly on through the moonlight, playing all the time on his bagpipe; the farther he went the more jolly he grew, and the squeaking tones of his bagpipe screamed shrill through the night air. When he had got to the middle of the heath, he saw huge blocks of stone that rose up in the pale moonlight, and not far from these were the dwellings of the dwarfs.

Leonard kept on playing louder and louder, till all at once he perceived a sound, at first like the soft murmur of a brook, then louder like the rushing of a torrent, and at last deep and fearful like the roar of the breakers. He could hear low, tittering laughs, suppressed whispers, and at length shuffling steps through the sand.

The piper held his breath. He thought all this very strange. He looked anxiously to the right and the left: the whole heath was alive and stirring, and moving in every direction with something, he could not see what, for the moon was just then covered by a cloud.

All at once the moon shone out, and Leonard cried out aloud with terror. On the right and on the left, before him and behind him, everywhere, as far as his eye could reach, the heath was covered with dwarfs, and all were rushing towards him.

Leonard turned back, and would have taken to his heels, but the dwarfs everywhere blocked up his way, and called out with their grasshopper-like voices: "This is the jolly piper, Leonard, who is come to play for us to dance."

Leonard struck about him, and tried to keep off the dwarfs, but they cried out, "You belong to us, and now you shall see come to pass what you have always declared should happen. Play up and dance with us."

All resistance was vain, an invisible power constrained him; he put the mouth-piece of the bagpipe to his lips, and began to play and to dance in spite of himself. The dwarfs whirled with him in a circle, and every time he tried to stop, they shouted, "Play away, jolly piper! Play and dance as we do!"

So it went on the whole night. But the paler grew the stars, the weaker grew the tones of the bagpipe, and Leonard could scarcely lift his feet from the ground; but when the day dawned and the cocks began to crow, the dwarfs vanished and all became still.

The jolly mountain piper fell breathless to the ground. The bagpipe dropped from his mouth, his hands fell powerless at his side, and his head sunk heavily upon his breast. All around him in the air resounded a kind of whispered song:

"Sleep, jolly piper, sleep! What you have so often sworn should happen, has come to pass. Your last moment was spent in music, dancing, and drunkenness."

When the people came in the morning to look for the piper, they found him lying dead on the heath. The meeting with the dwarfs had been his destruction.

—From *Popular Legends of Brittany* by Emile Souvestre, from a German translation by Heinrich Bode, translated into English by "A Lady," 1854.

—❖—

By the pipes of McGorrisk they danced and they sung,
Like divils, wid mad possessed;
And Father O'Toole, in the widow's embrace,
was shaking his foot wid the best.
From the traditional song "McFadden's Picnic"

The Piper Came to Our Town   239

I have power, high power for freedom,
    To wake the burning soul;
I have sonnets that through the ancient hills,
    Like a torrent's voice might roll;
I have pealing notes of victory,
    That might welcome kings from war;
I have rich deep tones to send the wail,
    for a hero's death afar.

CPSIA information can be obtained
at www.ICGtesting.com
Printed in the USA
FSHW02n2307130518
48177FS